POETRY AND SONG

scrap books

NATURE

FALL FIRES

Inventors

THE BIRDS FLY SOUTH

Fourth of July

GREAT EVENTS

baby birds

WOOD CUTTING

N · NE · E · SE · S · SW · W

Beethoven

SNOW ANGELS

GREAT MEN

Edison

THE WIND

PUMPKINS

CHRISTMAS

OUTDOORS

Santa Claus

MAY POLE

Pueblo Indians

STRANGE PEOPLE

masks

WITCHES

Jim McCoy

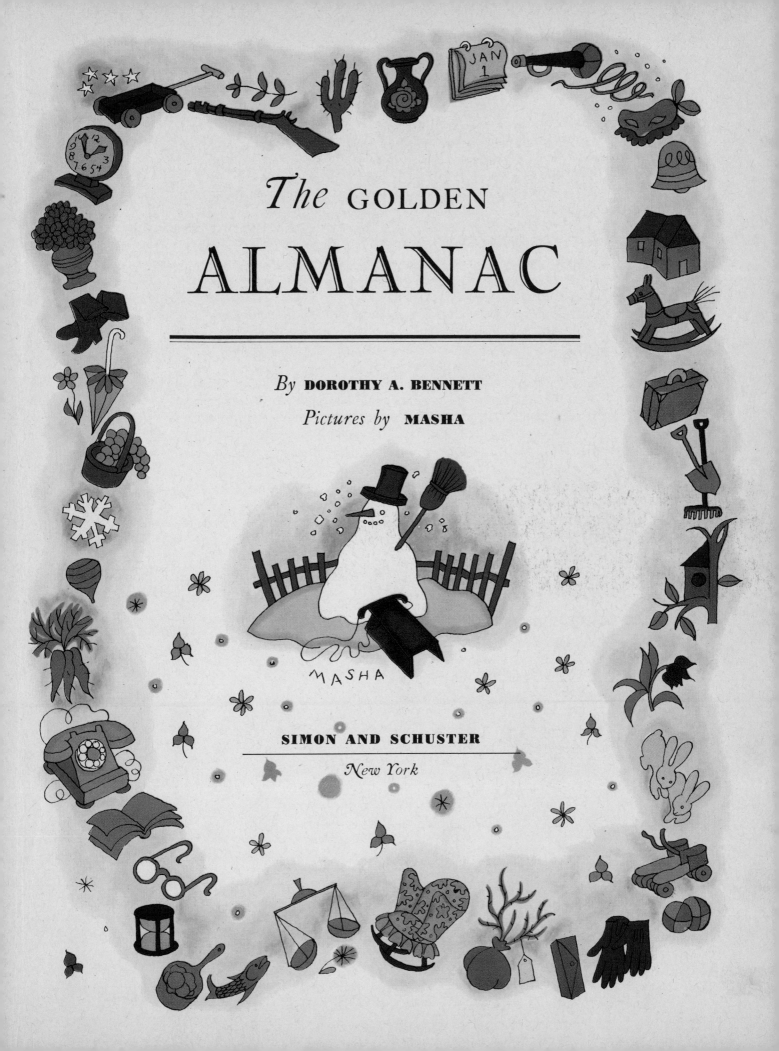

The GOLDEN
ALMANAC

By **DOROTHY A. BENNETT**

Pictures by **MASHA**

MASHA

SIMON AND SCHUSTER

New York

Acknowledgments:

D. Appleton-Century Company for "The War Dance of the Mice" from *Pueblo Indian Folk Stories* by Charles F. Lummis

Dodd, Mead and Company, Inc. for "Jack Frost" by Gabriel Setoun from *A Child's World*

Walt Disney Productions for "Winter" from the Disney motion picture adaptation of Felix Salten's *Bambi*.

Margaret Wise Brown for "September," "November," and "December" from her *The Children's Year*

Harcourt, Brace and Company, Inc. for "The Cat" from *Little Children* by William Saroyan, copyright, 1937, by Harcourt, Brace and Company, Inc.

Henry Holt and Company, Inc. for "The Fly" from *The Collected Poems of Walter De La Mare*, for "The Pasture" from *The Collected Poems of Robert Frost*, and for "Fog" from *Chicago Poems* by Carl Sandburg

Houghton-Mifflin Company for "The Story of the First Butterflies" from *Book of Nature Myths* by Holbrook

Lida for "Baby Bears' School" from her *Bruin the Brown Bear*, "Preparing for Winter" from her *Pompom the Little Red Squirrel*, "The Enchanted Garden" and "Spiky and the Gypsies" from her *Spiky the Hedgehog*

Little, Brown & Company for "Danny Meadow Mouse Plays Hide and Seek" from *The Adventures of Danny Meadow Mouse* by Thornton Burgess; and for "Will There Really Be A Morning" from *The Poems of Emily Dickinson*, edited by Martha Dickinson Bianchi and Alfred Leete Hampson; both reprinted by permission of Little, Brown & Company

The Macmillan Company for "At Night" and "Indian Summer" from *Rhymes About Ourselves* by Marchette Gaylord Chute

Random House for "Our Friends the Mice" from *Inhale and Exhale* by William Saroyan

Charles Scribner's Sons for "The Duck's Ditty" and "Winter in the Woods" from *The Wind in the Willows* by Kenneth Grahame

Simon and Schuster, Inc. for "Winter" from the Walt Disney motion picture adaptation of Felix Salten's *Bambi*.

Dorothy Brown Thompson for "Arbor Day" from *Celebrations for Festivals*, edited by Robert Haven Schauffler

TABLE OF CONTENTS

This Is an Almanac

EVERYONE knows that a clock tells the hours of the day, from one to twelve and round again. An almanac tells about the days of the months and the months of the year. It explains when and why we have day and night, winter and summer, snow and rain. It tells when the birds go south for the winter and when the flowers come up in the spring.

The SEASONS

WE KNOW by the clock that most people eat breakfast around seven or eight, and lunch about noon or twelve o'clock, and dinner or supper about six or seven. We think of the day as having two parts, morning and afternoon. And we often say that the night has two parts—the evening, and then the dark night.

The year is divided into four parts, also. The morning of the year is the spring, when the green grass appears and everything begins to wake up from its long winter sleep.

The afternoon of the year is the summer, when the sun is hot and the flowers and fruits appear in garden and field.

The evening, or twilight, of the year is autumn, when the days begin to grow short, and the leaves fall from the trees.

And winter is the deep night of the year, when the nights are long and cold and many plants and animals are at rest under the snow or deep in burrows under the ground.

Spring always begins in March and summer always in June. Autumn (some people call it fall) starts in late September and winter begins just before Christmas in December.

What Makes Night and Day

WHEN PEOPLE first lived on the earth they didn't have clocks. They guessed what time it was by looking at the sun. They didn't have a calendar, so they guessed at the time of the year by the warmth of the sun and the length of the days. They looked at the leaves on the trees and watched the birds and animals.

They were curious about many things and they often made up stories about why certain things happened.

They couldn't understand why we had day and night. They knew that when the sun came up it brought the day, and when the sun went down, it took the day away with it and left the

night instead. After a while they decided that the sun was a great ball of fire, or a big plate of gold. They decided that someone must either pull it up into the sky on a rope, or row it across the sky in a boat.

As the years went by they watched the sky more carefully, and finally decided that the sun was a great big ball of fire all right, but it was a long way away, millions of miles away, and much too big for anyone to pull or row around. Instead, it is the earth that moves.

The Earth Spins

The earth spins like a top. So first one side is turned toward the sun, then the other side. When our side of the earth first turns toward the sun, the sun appears to rise in the east. We get up and have breakfast. As the earth turns farther around, the sun seems to climb across the sky. When it gets up quite high, it is noon, and we eat lunch. Then the sun seems to roll down the sky during the afternoon while people are taking naps and going for walks. By supper time the sun is over in the west ready to roll out of sight for the evening. When it is all gone it grows dark out-of-doors and night begins for us.

But when the sun sets for our part of the world, it is rising for other people. And so as the earth spins like a top the sun rises and rolls across the sky and sets, and then rises somewhere else. So we have day and night, day and night for dozens, yes hundreds, even millions of days one after the other.

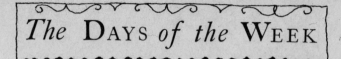

The Days of the Week

It would get very tiresome to try to keep track of the days unless we had some kind of system. So we named the days Monday, Tuesday, Wednesday, Thursday, Friday, Saturday, and Sunday. These seven days, we say, make a week. When they have gone by, we use them all over again, week after week, year after year.

The Months

Just the days of the week (Monday, Tuesday, Wednesday, Thursday, Friday, Saturday, and Sunday) and the seasons of the year (winter, spring, summer, and fall) are not enough to keep track of the days. Suppose you wanted to tell someone when your birthday is. (When is it, by the way?) You wouldn't want to say the seventh day of the seventh week of the winter, would you?

Long ago people divided the seasons into parts. There are twelve of them. They are the months and their names are January, February, March, April, May, June, July, August, September, October, November, December.

Indian Month Names

The Indians gave the months names which described them. Thus they have the months called—

JANUARY: *Snow Moon*
FEBRUARY: *Hunger Moon*
MARCH: *Crow Moon*
APRIL: *Wild Goose Moon*
MAY: *Planting Moon*
JUNE: *Song Moon*
JULY: *Thunder Moon*
AUGUST: *Green Corn Moon*
SEPTEMBER: *Harvest Moon*
OCTOBER: *Leaf-Falling Moon*
NOVEMBER: *Ice-Forming Moon*
DECEMBER: *Long Night Moon*

January

The first day of January is New Year's Day. In the northern states there is snow and ice, sliding and skating. The woods ring with the sound of the axe and the snow is laced with the scampering tracks of mice and squirrels. Oranges are ripe for picking in California, tomatoes in Texas, and grapefruit in Florida.

Snowflakes

IN JANUARY in most parts of the United States it is fairly cold, and in the northern half there is nearly always snow. Sometimes the snow falls at night while we are asleep. We wake up in the morning, look out the window, and discover that the whole ground is covered with a white blanket. Trees look as though they were painted with birthday cake frosting.

Other times a flurry of snow comes in the day-time when we are out walking. Then we can see the beautiful little flakes all made of the tiniest little crystals. There are millions and millions of them in a snowfall. Yet it seems as though no two are alike. Some snowflakes are round, and some are like stars. Some are all open and lacy, like valentines, and some are like the wing of a butterfly. Each is like a beautiful jewel.

Snowflakes are really made of the same tiny particles of moisture of which the rain is made— only we have snow when it is too cold for rain. Some of the tiny little particles of moisture that are in the air form wee little bars of ice. Drifting about in the air they pick up more particles of moisture that become ice crystals and build up a pattern. There are countless beautiful shapes and designs.

After a good many particles of moisture have been added, the snowflake is heavy enough so that it cannot float in the air, but must fall to the ground. Then it falls to roof and fence post, to prairie and playground.

When the snow falls in the city, it soon melts on the roofs and trees and is shoveled off the streets. In the parks where there is grass, it may last long enough for boys and girls to get out their sleds and have a good time sliding. Now and then it snows long enough so the snow is deep and lasts for days and days. Then there is time to play all kinds of games in it.

Things to Do

MAKING SNOW ANGELS

IF ONE is dressed warmly in a snow suit, it is fun to make angels in the snow. To do this you have to lie right down in the snow on your back, so you must have overshoes, long trousers, a warm coat, a wooly scarf, and a snug hat. Even then, if you are not careful, you may get a bit of snow down your neck.

First you pick a nice smooth place where no one has even walked in the snow. Then you lie down carefully with your arms stretched out to the sides. Move your arms up so they touch your ears and then down till they touch your sides. Do this three or four times; then get up ever so carefully. Try not to touch your hands outside of where you were lying, and step off carefully when you get to your feet. Then turn around and look down. You will see the outlines of a snow angel! For out beside the hollows made by your head and body and legs you will see great white wings.

Games to Play

Fox and Geese

A GAME that is fun to play in the snow if there are three or four boys and girls is Fox and Geese. You know a fox likes nothing better than a good fat goose to eat, and a goose is very anxious to stay out of the fox's way. So this is really a game of tag, but played in the snow a special way.

First you find a good big patch of snow that has no footmarks in it. Then you run around and make a big circle. Go around it often enough to make the circle deep and easy to see. Next, run across the circle, just as though it were a great big cake and you were the knife cutting it right through the middle. Then walk along the outside of the circle till you come to where you could cut it in half once again. And if you have a big circle, you can cut it in eight pieces.

Now you are ready to play tag. Someone must be "it," of course. Maybe since you are the one who will be telling the other children how to play the game, you should be "it" the first time.

It is your job to try to catch up with one of the other children and touch (or tag) him. All of the players can run only where you have cut the snow-pie. So around and around, and through and across you will run, until finally you catch one of them.

Then it is his turn to be "it" and to chase the other children. Of course you can play this game with just two, but it is much more fun to have three or four.

Making Snow Figures

IF THE snow is nice and sticky, it is fun to make little balls and roll them into great big balls. Maybe you will want to make a house of them, or put one on top of the other and make a snow man. If you can borrow a broom and an old hat, find two or three pieces of coal and an old tie, you can make a very handsome snow man.

Sometime you may be able to make a snow image of your dog, or of a squirrel, or a rabbit. Rolls of newspaper or sticks of wood will help make the legs and tail. It is easier if you make the animals lying down.

Snow Tracks

IF YOU are in the country or even in the city park, you may see a real rabbit, or at least his tracks in the snow. For rabbits and squirrels and birds and mice come out and scamper over the deep snow.

The rabbit makes a very handsome track as he jumps. You can always tell where his front feet and his hind feet hit.

Rabbit tracks are very different from the tracks of a cat. The cat walks daintily one foot after the other and you can always tell in which direction she was going.

You may see where a dog walked or ran through the snow. His prints are different from all the others.

The Indians knew all the animals by their tracks. In fact they could often tell what tribe an Indian belonged to just by looking at his tracks. They noticed how the moccasins (or soft shoes) were made. Each tribe made their moccasins a little different, and so their tracks were different, too.

The place to look for the squirrel's tracks is by a tree. You can usually see where he jumped off the trunk, landed in the snow, and then went jumping on. He lands with his four feet quite close together and his tracks look very different from either the dog or the cat, and they are different from the rabbit's, too.

Mice are the most fun to look for because their tracks are so very tiny—four little footmarks quite close together, much smaller than the squirrels. Often they have little tunnels under the snow. Sometimes the door of one of these tunnels comes up beside a clump of dried brown grass. Sometimes the tunnel ends beside a big rock. So if you look closely you may see a very small hole in the snow and then off in some direction away from it a scamper of tiny footmarks.

Morning

Will there really be a morning?
Is there such a thing as day?
Could I see it from the mountains
If I were as tall as they?

Has it feet like water-lilies?
Has it feathers like a bird?
Is it brought from famous countries
Of which I have never heard?

Oh, some scholar! Oh, some sailor!
Oh, some wise man from the skies!
Please to tell a little pilgrim
Where the place called morning lies.

EMILY DICKINSON

Winter Woodcutting

Out in the country, boys and girls help with the winter chores. One of the best things is to help with the wood chopping. Perhaps Father will make a sled to haul the winter's wood on.

First of all he must find the right kind of trees. This means walking through the snowy woods, until finally Father finds the right oak for the pole, two straight maples for the runners, and a good knotless ash for the cross-pieces. You know that wherever there is a branch on a tree it makes a round hard place we call a knot in the wood. So Father looks for a tree without any low branches.

Then comes the wonderful sound of the ax as it sings into the tree. The chips begin to fly. Now Father steps to the other side and makes a cut there too. "Stand back, children," he calls, "over there by the little green fir tree."

There is a tearing sound, and then a sharp crack as the trunk breaks off, and then sharp snappings as branches break with the fall, and there lies the tree. "Now to find the next one," says Father, and off they go.

After all the trees have been cut, it is time to go back and get the horse to haul them to the barn to be sawed. Then the fun of making the sled begins. The bark must come off, the pieces must be cut, the runners be steamed to bend easily, and the screws soaped to turn smoothly.

When the sled is done, the winter's wood-cutting is really just started. There will be wood chopping for days, even weeks. Boys and girls may pick up bark, carry chips, and pile pieces out beside the barn. They may watch while the sled is loaded, help with the unloading up by the house, and, of course, carry wood for the kitchen every day.

✳☆✳☆ Stargazing ☆✳☆✳

Nighttime comes so early in January that sometimes you may be able to see some of the stars before going to bed.

There is a famous hunter whose picture is in the sky. You might look for him some evening. His name is Orion.

He has a very bright star in each shoulder, three bright ones to show where his belt is, and two more to show where his feet are. You can even see his sword hanging down from his belt.

Right behind him are his two hunting dogs, a big one and a little one. Each of them has a bright star right on the tip of his nose.

To find the hunter, look in the east. You know how to find the east, don't you? That is where you first see the sun in the morning, on the other side of the sky from where the sun sets in the afternoon.

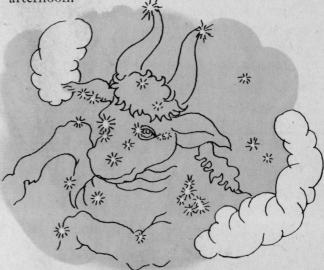

Don't forget to look for the great big animal that Orion is following across the sky. His name is Taurus and he is a bull. He has a fierce red eye, and on one shoulder he has a beautiful little patch of stars that looks almost like a soup ladle. You can easily see six of these, and if you look very hard you may be able to see one more.

This tiny little patch of stars the ancient people of Greece called the Seven Sisters or The Pleiades. The American Indians called it the Six Brothers.

If you do find these stars before you go to bed, then ask some grownups to tell you next day how Orion looked when *they* went to bed. For, just like the sun, the stars seem to roll across the sky forever and ever. They rise every night and go out of sight every morning. So Orion and his dogs were much higher in the sky when the grownups went to bed. And he dropped out of sight in the west just before you got up in the morning.

The First Balloon Flight

MANY INTERESTING and exciting things have happened in January in other years.

In January nearly one hundred and fifty years ago (before your father, or your grandfather, your great-grandfather, or great-great-grandfather was born) the first man went up in a balloon, in the United States. Way back in 1793 he went way up into the clouds in a basket attached to a big balloon. Until that day, people thought that such a thing could not be done.

Discovery of Pluto

A VERY exciting thing happened in January, too, when a new world was discovered.

Did you know there are other worlds, very much like our earth? One of them you may see looking like a bright star in the sky. Perhaps your mother or father, or aunt or uncle has pointed it out to you. Maybe they said, "See the evening star." It looked like a star, but it was probably the planet Venus. And there is another planet near us too. It is called Mercury. Then far away from the earth are Mars and Jupiter and Saturn.

One day, looking through telescopes which make everything look bigger, some men found two more worlds that were too far away to be seen with just eyes. They called these Uranus and Neptune. And then one day in January in 1930, an astronomer found another world. This one he called Pluto.

All these worlds move around the sun, just as our earth does. There are nine planets in the sun's family. They all get their light from the sun. They have day and night as they spin like tops, like the earth, too.

January Birthday

SOME INTERESTING people have their birthdays in January. Do you know about BENJAMIN FRANKLIN? He was an amazing man who lived in George Washington's time. That was long ago when the United States of America was a little, new country.

Benjamin Franklin could do almost anything. He believed that if you wanted to do something or to make something, you could do it. He could print newspapers, edit magazines (he started the *Saturday Evening Post*), make laws, and talk to foreign kings, and he wrote an almanac, too. In fact he did so many interesting things that many books have been written about him. He was born on January 17.

The Fairies

Up the airy mountain,
  Down the rushy glen,
We daren't go a-hunting
  For fear of little men;
Wee folk, good folk,
  Trooping all together;
Green jacket, red cap,
  And white owl's feather.

Down along the rocky shore
  Some make their home,
They live on crispy pancakes
  Of yellow tide-foam;
Some in the reeds
  Of the black mountain lake,
With frogs for their watch-dogs,
  All night awake.

High on the hill-top
  The old king sits;
He is now so old and gray
  He's nigh lost his wits.
With a bridge of white mist
  Columbkill he crosses,

On his stately journeys
  From Slieveleague to Rosses;
Or going up with music
  On cold starry nights
To sup with the Queen
  Of the gay northern lights.

By the craggy hill-side,
  Through the mosses bare,
They have planted thorn-trees
  For pleasure here and there.
If any man so daring
  As dig them up in spite,
He shall find their sharpest thorns
  In his bed at night.

Up the airy mountain,
  Down the rushy glen,
We daren't go a-hunting
  For fear of little men;
Wee folk, good folk,
  Trooping all together;
Green jacket, red cap,
  And white owl's feather.

WILLIAM ALLINGHAM

February

Frosty days make February a wintry month. There is fishing through the ice on the frozen northern lakes, and ice to be cut and stored for summer days. The sun sets early and the days are short. The month is short too, but it has two holidays to honor famous heroes, and Valentine's Day besides.

VALENTINE'S DAY

FEBRUARY 14 is Valentine's Day. On this day we send valentines to people we like. Sometimes they send us valentines, too. It is fun to get them; it is fun to send them; but most of all it is fun to make valentines.

To make valentines you will need colored papers, pencil, crayons, scissors with blunt points, paste, and perhaps an old magazine that you may cut up.

Most valentines have hearts on them, and flowers, and a message. They may say "Be my valentine" or "I love you" or "Will you be mine?"

Here are two easy valentines to make:

1. Draw a heart on a sheet of white paper and a bigger one on a sheet of red paper. Cut them both out. Write one of the valentine messages given above on the white heart, and draw bright-colored flowers all around it with your crayons. Paste the white heart onto the red heart.

2. Cut a piece of colored paper (red is the most popular valentine color but others are pretty too) about four inches by six inches—big enough so that when you fold it once it makes a nice little book. Find a pretty picture in an old magazine or draw one with crayons; cut it out and paste it on the front of the valentine. Write a valentine message inside the book and sign your name.

When you have made these two valentines you will want to try others all your own.

Ice Magic

WHEN FEBRUARY begins, there is still winter in the air. Even where there is not much snow, there is nearly always frost. Tiny ice crystals coat the tree trunks and hang like feathers from the telephone wires. They decorate the brown weeds with sparkling spangles and make even automobiles look as though they had been sprayed with star dust. Window panes and store windows have beautiful designs and fantastic landscapes. At night the moon shines on a silver world and the morning sun makes everything sparkle like diamonds.

The MOON

THE MOON gives its name to the month. We really should say *moonth*. But month seems easier to say and sounds a little better to our ears, so we say *month* instead.

Long ago the ancients discovered that the moon was as regular as a clock and could be used for telling time, too. Of course the face of the clock shows twelve hours; but the face of the moon tells more than two times that many *days*.

How? Well, you know the moon sometimes looks like a cookie just out of the oven, and sometimes it looks broken in half, and sometimes it looks like a curl of orange peel. If you count the days while its face is changing, you will discover that it always takes the same amount of time to make these changes. So the faces make a good measuring stick.

The moon is like the earth, only smaller. The sun shines on it just as it does on the earth. So one side of the moon has day and one side has night, just as on the world. From our place here on earth we can sometimes see all of the daylight side of the moon. Then it looks like a whole cookie or a dinner plate. But the moon travels around the earth. So sometimes the dark side is turned toward us, and we see only a sliver of the lighted side.

The YEAR

FOR MANY years people just used the moon months to keep track of time. When twelve full moons had passed they said the year was over and they began a new one with the next full moon.

There was one trouble with that way of measuring the year. It meant there were always a few extra days left over. There are really 365 days in the year. Twelve moon months didn't quite use up that many.

The year is another thing that is measured by something that happens in the sky. You remember that the day is 24 hours long because that is the time it takes the earth to spin on its axis like a top (through daylight and night, back to daylight again). The month is about 30 days long because that is the time that it takes the moon to go around the earth (from new moon to evening crescent,

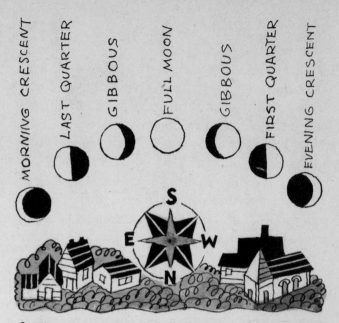

first quarter, gibbous, full moon, gibbous, last quarter to new moon again). The year is really 365 days long because that is the time it takes the earth to go around the sun (through winter, spring, summer, and fall back to winter again).

Just think of it! How smoothly and steadily the earth must move so that we never notice any jiggling or any sign that it is spinning and rolling. To think that it spins like a top and rolls around the sky—and we cannot feel it at all! But we can see it happen. That is how the astronomers found out about it. They watched and watched. They figured and figured. And finally they figured it all out for us.

The year is 365 days and 12 moon months don't quite need that many days. There were always some left over. To make everything come out even the extra days were passed around to the months. But there were not enough to go all around, so it came out this way:

Thirty days has September,
April, June and November,
All the rest have thirty-one.
February has twenty-eight alone,
Excepting Leap Year, that's the time
When February's days are twenty-nine.

Every fourth year is called Leap Year, and has one extra day. That arrangement works very well and our calendar has been like this for more than two hundred years.

A Toy Circus

FEBRUARY is a good month to have your own circus. Get out all the animals you have among your toys. Cut pictures out of magazines and mount them on cardboard.

Make a circus ring out of a jumping rope or a wall of books. Then have a parade with all the animals lined up. If you have some wagons and carts or trains they can carry some of the animals just the way they do in a real circus. Dolls can be the ring masters, clowns, tumblers, and trapeze artists.

When you have practiced your parade and have your dolls fixed so that there is something for them to do in the circus rings, you might have a regular circus show. You could ask some of your playmates and some older people too. Your playmates might bring some of their animals to add to the parade.

There is a good song to sing when the animals are on parade. It goes like this: "The animals came in two by two." Perhaps you can learn to sing it.

The song tells about the time when there was a great flood. Noah built an ark to keep the animals from drowning. You could make an ark out of a box and have your animals get aboard after the circus is over.

One More River

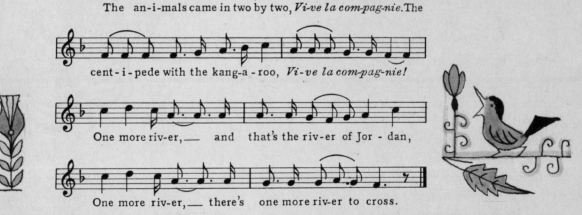

The an-i-mals came in two by two, *Vi-ve la com-pag-nie.* The
cent-i-pede with the kang-a-roo, *Vi-ve la com-pag-nie!*
One more riv-er,— and that's the riv-er of Jor-dan,
One more riv-er,— there's one more riv-er to cross.

The animals came in three by three,
  Vive la compagnie.
The elephant on the back of the flea,
  Vive la compagnie.
    One more river, etc.

The animals came in four by four,
  Vive la compagnie.
The camel, he got stuck in the door,
  Vive la compagnie.
    One more river, etc.

There was a long war but finally Washington's army won. The colonies became the United States of America. Washington became the first president.

ABRAHAM LINCOLN

Abraham Lincoln was the sixteenth president of the United States. There was a great war in his time, too. It was the Civil War. The Civil War was fought between the Americans of the southern states, who wanted to leave the Union, and the Americans of the northern states, who wanted to keep the United States together. The north, or

Two Birthdays

THE TWO most famous men who ever lived in America were born in February. They were such important men that we have holidays on their birthdays and all kinds of celebrations. They were George Washington and Abraham Lincoln. You can see Lincoln's picture on a penny, and Washington's is on a postage stamp; Lincoln's is on the five-dollar bill, Washington's on the dollar bill.

GEORGE WASHINGTON

George Washington was the first general in the American army. He led the Colonies in the Revolutionary War against England way back in 1776.

The people in the colonies came mostly from England, but they did not want England to rule them in this country. So they wrote the Declaration of Independence and told England that they wanted to govern themselves.

Union army won. The southern states did not leave the union. During the war all the slaves in the United States were freed. For this Lincoln will always be famous.

If Candlemas-day [Feb. 2] be dry and fair
The half of winter's to come and mair:
If Candlemas-day be wet and foul
The half of winter's gane at Yule.

January brings the snow,
Makes our feet and fingers glow.

February brings the rain,
Thaws the frozen lake again.

March brings breezes loud and shrill,
Stirs the dancing daffodil.

April brings the primrose sweet,
Scatters daisies at our feet.

May brings flocks of pretty lambs,
Skipping by their fleecy dams.

June brings tulips, lilies, roses,
Fills the children's hands with posies.

Hot July brings cooling showers,
Apricots and gillyflowers.

August brings the sheaves of corn,
Then the harvest home is borne.

Warm September brings the fruit,
Sportsmen then begin to shoot.

Fresh October brings the pheasant,
Then to gather nuts is pleasant.

Dull November brings the blast,
Then the leaves are whirling fast.

Chill December brings the sleet,
Blazing fire and Christmas treat.

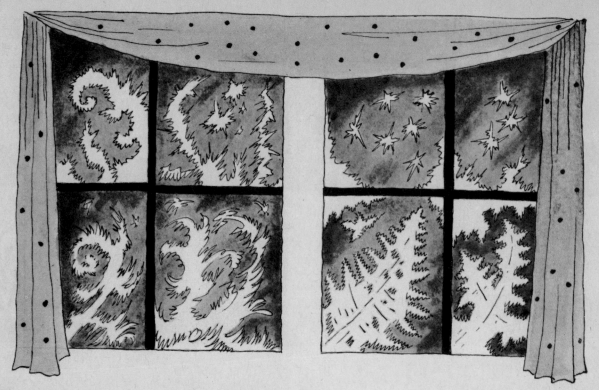

Jack Frost

The door was shut as doors should be
   Before you went to bed last night,
Yet Jack Frost has got in, you see,
   And left your windows silver white.

He must have waited till you slept;
   And not a single word he spoke,
But pencilled o'er the panes and crept
   Away again before you woke.

And now you cannot see the hills
   Nor fields that stretch beyond the lane;
But there are fairer things than these
   His fingers traced on every pane.

Rocks and castles towering high;
   Hills and dales, and streams and fields;
And knights in armour riding by,
   With nodding plumes and shining shields.

And here are little boats, and there
   Big ships with sails spread to the breeze;
And yonder palm trees waving fair
   On islands set in silver seas.

And butterflies with gauzy wings;
   And herds of cows and flocks of sheep;
And fruit and flowers and all the things
   You see when you are fast asleep.

For creeping softly underneath
   The door when all the lights are out,
Jack Frost takes every breath you breathe,
   And knows the things you think about.

He paints them on the window pane
   In fairy lines with frozen steam
And when you wake you see again
   The lovely things you saw in dream.

GABRIEL SETOUN

The Moon

The moon has a face like the clock in the hall;
She shines on thieves on the garden wall,
On streets and fields and harbour quays,
And birdies asleep in the forks of the trees.

The squalling cat and the squeaking mouse,
The howling dog by the door of the house,
The bat that lies in bed at noon,
All love to be out by the light of the moon.

But all of the things that belong to the day
Cuddle to sleep to be out of the way;
And flowers and children close their eyes
Till up in the morning the sun shall rise.

ROBERT LOUIS STEVENSON

Playing Astronomer

IF YOU HAVE two balls, or an orange and a grapefruit, a big plate and a lamp, you can see just how the moon changes. You can pretend to be an astronomer.

Turn on the lamp and pretend it's the sun. Now take the big ball and put it on the plate where the lamplight shines on it.

Pretend that is the world where we live. You can even mark the place where your house is, if you want to. The side of the ball toward the lamp is bright and the side away from it is dark. The light side is the daylight side, the dark side the night side.

Now take the other ball. Hold it on the edge of the plate near the earth and see how it has day and night, too. Now the big ball is the earth. The little ball is the moon.

Roll the "moon" ball around the edge of the plate out beyond the "earth" ball on the side away from the "sun." That's the way the sun, earth, and moon are out in the sky, when we see a *full moon*. All the lighted part of the moon, the day side, is turned toward the earth.

Now roll the small ball along the edge of the plate around the big ball. This is the way the moon travels around the earth. As it moves around toward the sun, from our place on the earth we see less and less of the daylight side of the moon. It shrinks and shrinks day after day. Soon it is just half a cookie and finally it is nibbled so close to the edge that we can hardly see it at all.

Once in a while you can see it in the daytime if you look carefully. And finally when it is just in between the sun and the earth (the big ball and the lamp) none of its daylight side is toward the earth at all. Then from the earth we cannot see the moon anywhere in the sky. This, and also the first sliver to reappear, is called the *new moon*.

It takes about a week from full cookie to half, and it takes another week from half cookie to no cookie at all. Then in another week there is another half cookie. In one week more, there is a full moon again. So from a big shining full moon around to a full moon again takes some four weeks, or about thirty days. That is the way the month was first measured.

[25]

March

The wintry days end in March and the windy days begin then. Blustery gusts whirl people's hats through the streets, blow papers up to second story windows, and turn umbrellas inside out. It's maple sugar time in New England, and in Kentucky they are breaking and training colts. Spring begins as the days grow longer.

Winds

IT SEEMS STRANGE that the air we cannot see can push so strongly. We can see when it pushes the clouds, and when it swirls dust from the streets. We can see it blow the flags on their poles and the sails of ships at sea. We can see it turn the windmills of the farmers and carry the seeds of trees and flowers. But usually we can only *feel* air.

The weather man tells us that when the sun heats the ground the heated air rises. You know how the flame of a match or a candle always goes up. No matter how they are held the flames always go up. And over a fire or a radiator you can see the disturbance made by the heated air rising.

As the hot air goes up, cold air drops down to take its place. And as they change and push into each other's places—that is what makes the wind.

> When the wind is in the east,
> 'Tis neither good for man or beast;
> When the wind is in the north,
> The skillful fisher goes not forth;
> When the wind is in the south,
> It blows the bait in fishes' mouth;
> When the wind is in the west,
> Then 'tis at the very best.

The ZODIAC

LONG AGO the ancients marked a belt in the sky made of animal pictures. There are a lion and a bull, and a fish and a scorpion, and a goat and a ram. They called this circus ring the Zodiac.

They found that always after the sun went down, the sun's place was in some part of that belt of stars, and its place was constantly changing among the animals of the Zodiac.

The sun has a regular place to be for each month of the year. As the earth rolls round the sun with the year, it makes the sun's place seem to change. We say it is in a different "sign of the Zodiac."

If you watch the stars at sunset, you can tell the season of the year from that just as well as from the calendar or from the way the weather feels.

Easter

EASTER sometimes comes in March. That is the day when the Easter bunnies and the Easter eggs are hidden away. If you look very carefully in all the corners of the rooms or under the porch, or out in the park under the bushes, you may be able to find some pretty colored eggs. There may even be an Easter basket. But the bunnies are so busy they cannot always get baskets and eggs to all children, so do not be too disappointed if he didn't get to you this time.

Making Easter Eggs

EASTER EGGS are fun to make. Mother will hard-boil some eggs for you and set them away to cool. When they are cool you can decorate them. Water color paints make pretty colored eggs. With crayons you can do lots of different things —draw pictures or make fancy colored patterns.

Try drawing faces on some of the eggs. Draw hair on top of the egg and make a little round collar of paper pasted in a circle for the head to stand on.

SPRING

SPRING begins on March 21 as a rule. On that date the sun rises exactly in the east, and sets exactly in the west, and there are just 12 hours from sunrise to sunset and 12 hours from sunset to sunrise again. You remember how long the nights were in winter and how short the days. In spring the nights and days are more nearly the same, or equal. In fact, this first day of spring is called the day of the equinox—because that word means equal night and day.

✳☆ THE SUN OVERHEAD ☆✳

IF ON THIS DAY you could take an airplane to Ecuador in South America, to Lake Victoria in Africa, or to Borneo in the South China Sea, you would see something interesting. At noon you would see the sun exactly overhead in the very top of the sky. There are only two days in the year when this can happen—March 21 and September 21—the first day of spring and the first day of fall.

Those places are on the earth's equator. And the equator is a belt around the middle of the earth that divides it into two equal halves. You can put a string around an orange and see how it works. The halves are the northern hemisphere and the southern hemisphere. People in the United States live in the northern hemisphere.

On March 21 the sun is shining equally on both halves. That is why it is right in the top of the sky at the equator on that day. But as the earth goes round the sun day after day several changes take place.

✳☆ THE EARTH ON ITS AXIS ☆✳

THE REASON IS THIS: the earth is a bit tipsy. Yes, that's right, it's tipsy: it is tipped over a bit. The astronomer says it is tipped on its axis.

The axis is what the earth turns on, like the axle of a wheel. And the earth is tipped on its axis to the path in which it moves around the sun. So as it goes on around the sun after March 21,

the sun shines more and more on the northern half. That makes the days longer and warmer.

Each day the sun rises a little bit farther north of the east point, it climbs higher at noon and has a longer journey to make across the sky. And it sets farther to the north of the west point. Of course you have to watch the sky very closely to see all of those things happen. Mostly the astronomers do the watching and tell us what happens.

Who Has Seen the Wind?

Who has seen the wind?
 Neither I nor you:
But when the leaves hang trembling,
 The wind is passing through.

Who has seen the wind?
 Neither you nor I:
But when the trees bow down their heads,
 The wind is passing by.

CHRISTINA GEORGINA ROSETTI

Maple Sugaring

Sunshiny days in March tell us that spring is on the way. A patch of green may appear here and there through the snow. But more snow may come later.

Then will come an especially bright day in March when the bark of the trees will glisten black and moist in the sun. The sap stored down in the roots of the trees all winter will start to rise. This is maple sugar time in New England and some other northeastern states — one of the most exciting times of the year.

Out come the drills, the spouts, the pails, the covers. The horses are harnessed and hitched to the sled. Out come mittens and mufflers and deep snow boots. Every one in the family gets ready for work and for fun. Off to the sugar orchard go fathers and mothers, aunts and uncles, and boys and girls. Many hands will be busy for many days making the sap of the maple trees into thick delicious syrup for pancakes and waffles.

Tapping the Trees

Father bores the up-slanting holes into the trees about little-finger deep. Into these he puts the spouts. A spout may be a plain tube carved of hard wood or a fancy one pressed from iron. Out of the spout the sap runs. Onto each spout the children hang a pail to catch the sap. And on the pail they put a cover, to keep out falling twigs or insects.

Everyone must work hard and fast. For when the sun warms the ground and the tree trunks, and the sap starts up from the roots, nothing but a very icy cold day can stop it! The sap rises steadily up in the roots, up the trunk, along the branches, out to the very tips of the twigs. And to make maple syrup, the sap must be drained off on its way up the trunk.

So it's rush, rush, rush, once the sap has started to rise, drill, drill, drill. Put in spout, put in spout. Hang on pail, hang on pail. Put on cover, put on cover. And start all over with more and more trees. There may be dozens, hundreds, even a thousand trees for one family to tend. It may be long after dark before they can stop to go home to dinner and to bed.

Gathering the Sap

The next day the children go from tree to tree to see how the sap is filling the pails. They may even drink a little of the sap from one of the spouts on the way. Imagine going up to a tree fountain and drinking maple syrup! Of course it isn't very syrupy yet, but it is sweet and good. It is just like having a private soda fountain right in your own back yard.

Father and his helpers come around and empty the buckets into the big tank on the sled. From tree to tree they go all day long. When the big tank is full, the sled starts off for the sugar house.

Just an ordinary tree may give ten gallons of syrup before the sap stops running. But even this sap makes only about one quart of syrup. For it must be cooked down, and down, and down to become thick and sweet and good.

Boiling Down the Syrup

In the sugar house the fires have been lighted and there are crackling logs and red-hot ashes under the big trays. Into these trays the men empty the sap. Then the fun begins. The steam begins to rise, and pretty soon the sap begins to boil. Bubbles tumble over one another right up to the very edge of the big trays. The sweet smell of the syrup seems to fill every nook and cranny of the sugar house and even all outdoors.

Of course the syrup must be tested. Mother will pour out some hot syrup onto the cold snow to cool. Perhaps there will be pickles and doughnuts to eat with it.

There may be some pans to lick after the candy is made, too, for maple sugar cream makes the *best* candies when it is poured into little molds shaped like leaves and acorns and balls and bats.

Birds and Animals in March

WHEN maple sugar time comes there are many other signs of spring appearing. Out in the country the woodchucks are up and about after their long winter rest. Out in the woods the raccoons and the bears wake up and poke their noses out to see if spring is really at hand.

Over the city and country the geese fly on their way back to the north. You can sometimes see their V-shaped patterns in the sky and hear their honk, honk, honk, from way above the roof tops and the trees.

An early robin or bluebird may have returned from the south and be out hunting for a place to build a nest.

April

Fresh green grass, bursting buds, tiny new leaves, and tender shoots bring spring to town and country. It's time for April Fool jokes and April fun indoors and out. It's time to watch for birds returning from the south, and in the country there are new baby lambs.

APRIL FOOL'S DAY

LAST APRIL FOOL'S DAY Stevie said to his mother, "Oh—there is a mouse right beside your foot." His mother said, "Oooooh!" and jumped up on the chair. Then Stevie laughed and said, "April Fool! There really isn't any mouse!"

Once Joby said to his sister Penny when they were in the park on April Fool's Day, "Look! there's a great big tiger right behind that rock. He must have escaped from the zoo." Penny jumped and ran to hide behind a tree. Then Joby laughed and said, "Ha! Ha! April Fool. There really isn't any tiger there at all."

On that same April Fool's Day Archer called to Dereck and said, "Oh, Dereck, look at that great big spider on the wall. Will you please get him down?" Dereck didn't like the big spiders in Florida any too well either, but he peeked out around the corner to see what he could do. Then Archer laughed and said, "April Fool, Dereck, there really isn't any spider, but thank you for being so brave and willing to catch it."

April Fool's is the day when you can make up any kind of story you want to. Tell it as seriously as you can. Then everyone will laugh when you remember to say, "April Fool."

April Fun

APRIL is the month for all kinds of fun. It is time for flying kites and playing tag and baseball. And many things are happening out-of-doors to the plants and animals. The buds on the trees are beginning to swell and burst. The pussy willows are strung like fuzzy little kittens all along the branches of the willow shrubs.

The squirrels are eating the last of their winter supply of nuts. Crocuses are up in the park. The robins, bluebirds, and the wrens and many other birds are building their nests.

Birds' Nests

MAYBE you can watch some bird making its nest. You will see it fly away and then come back with something in its bill. It may be a twig, or feather, or string, or grass. All kinds of things may be woven into that house in the tree, or under the eaves. Each kind of bird has its own way of building a nest.

The big straggling crow's nest of large twigs and leaves is very different from the beautifully woven swinging cradle of the oriole. The tiny hummingbird's little nest hardly bigger than a thimble is entirely different from the tunnels in the banks of lake or river that the kingfisher builds. If you watch closely when you see a nest, you will be able to tell what kind of bird it belongs to.

April Showers

THE STREETS and roads, parks and fields are often wet and shining in April, for it is the month of rain showers. People often say, "April showers bring May flowers." So we are glad to have it rain.

The longer sunshiny days warm the earth, the lakes, and the rivers. The melting snow runs off in rivulets, brooks, and streams and fills the lakes fuller and makes the rivers higher. Some of the moisture from the melting snow rises with the warm air riding on tiny specks of dust. Floating along through the air one particle of moisture joins another.

Great crowds of such little particles of moisture make the clouds. If the clouds get jostled by the wind, or if the little particles of moisture get big and heavy, down they come in drops of rain.

The rain is falling all around,
It falls on field and tree,
It rains on the umbrellas here,
And on the ships at sea.

ROBERT LOUIS STEVENSON

Arbor Day

To plant a tree! How small the twig,
And I beside it—very big.
A few years pass; and now the tree
Looks down on very little me.
A few years more—it is so high
Its branches seem to touch the sky.
I did not know that it would be
So vast a thing to plant a tree.

DOROTHY BROWN THOMPSON

Rainbows

SOMETIMES if the sun shines when it is raining you can see a rainbow. It is a beautiful sight. Be sure to look for one every time the sun shines when it is raining.

This is the way you can find one: First look toward the sun to see where it is in the sky. (But never look right into the sun. It is much too bright and it will hurt your eyes.) Then turn around so that the sun is at your back. Out there, in the opposite direction from the sun, you may see a rainbow. It will have red, orange, yellow, green, blue, and violet bands in it. And that rainbow is your *very own*, because no two people ever see exactly the same one.

Baby Bears' School

LITTLE BEARS have a great many things to learn while they are growing up.

The wise old bears of long ago had divided the school course for the young into two years.

During the first year the little bears should learn to

Play	Eat Properly
Climb	Dig
Listen	Wrestle
Sniff	Swim
Sharpen Claws	Run

School—The forest.

Hours—There were no hours. The little bears learned as they went along.

Teaching—Mamma set the example and Gruff saw to it that it was followed.

Discipline—If the bears were naughty or did their lesson upside down, Gruff cuffed them with his paw, but it was Mamma who punished them for really serious offenses.

Plush did not keep after her children all the time, saying, "Hold still," "Run around," "Come here," "Go away," "Answer me," or "Be quiet." Polka and Bruin were allowed to play as they liked—except in case of danger.

Plush encouraged them to be brave by licking the nose of the most daring.

But if Bruin tried to slip away from the group for one minute when her back was turned, his mother's paw would send him sprawling fifteen feet; and Gruff, for not being on the watch, would get a blow which landed him in the bushes head first with all four paws in the air.

"Perhaps that will teach you to look after your brother!" Plush would call after him.

So long as a little bear stays close to his mother no harm will come to him, but if he is alone and unprotected, he may fall in with bad company . . .

a hungry wolf, for instance. That is the reason Plush guarded her babies constantly. When they went for a walk she ambled ahead with Bruin on the right side and Polka on the left. Gruff followed close behind.

During their second year, young bears were taught to rely upon themselves. Polka and Bruin learned to hunt for their own food and to find their way about alone. They began to know which plants and animals could be eaten for food, which plants were useful as medicine, and which plants were not to be eaten at all because they were not good for bears.

That was when Bruin was grateful for the "gift of smell" he had acquired when he was very young.

His long nose seemed to know that tufts of grass between stones and roots were signs of delicious young shoots of beechnut trees and hazelnut flowers. This magnificent nose also informed him about the occupants of dark holes—here a fox, there a badger. Pooh! This must be a mole. (Ho! ho! ho! ho! dig and find out!) And again his wonderful nose told him that a wild pig followed by a flock of baby pigs had passed through this thicket! . . . a deer and her fawn had gone by, over there!

With such a nose, an intelligent bear may close his eyes and know, even in the middle of the night, the different saps in trees and all the different kinds of pine cones, herbs, and grasses. He can distinguish—and it isn't easy—between a green strawberry and a ripe one; a wilted daisy and a daisy in bud. But Bruin did even better than that! After sniffing about a bit, he could tell in advance just where a cluster of juicy mushrooms were pushing up through the earth. Or, again, he would catch the wet smell of an otter drying himself far off on the river bank.

from BRUIN, the Brown Bear by Lida

ARBOR DAY

APRIL is a good time to plant trees, because the ground is soft enough for the roots to push out. Then they can suck in water and minerals and all kinds of good things from the soil to feed the tree. And the days are warm enough to pull the sap up from the roots out to the tips of the branches and help the tree to grow.

So in April many trees are planted, especially on April tenth. That day is called Arbor Day or Tree Day. *Arbor* is an old word that means tree.

Maybe you can plant a tree this April. How about getting an orange or a grapefruit seed and planting it in a pot or in a window box? Or if you have an acorn or a maple seed, maybe you could find a place in the lawn or park to plant it. At school they may have little pine trees for the children to plant; then you may be able to plant a Christmas tree!

Do you know the tree that the acorn comes from? Do you know what the maple seed looks like? The acorn comes from the oak tree. The maple seed looks like the wing of a bird or the propeller of an airplane.

Can you tell a maple leaf from an oak leaf? Can you tell a willow leaf from an apple leaf? When you have a chance to do so, collect some leaves. Paste them into a scrap book, and write their names under them. Look at them closely. Is one short and wide? Is one long and narrow? Does one have sharp points on its edge like teeth? Or does it have big lobes like the fingers of your hands? Soon you will be able to recognize trees from their leaves.

Many of the things we use every day are made from trees. Your bed may be made from maple. Your play table or book cases may be pine. Your

dining room table or library desk may be made of oak. Your living-room chairs and tables may be walnut or mahogany.

The newspapers we see every day and our magazines are also made from wood. The wood in them was cut in chunks, then ground very fine, washed and strained, and rolled very thin.

Strange as it sounds, your mother's stockings are probably made from wood. That seems very hard to believe, but rayon is made from wood. The wood is chopped fine, cooked into something almost like syrup, forced through tiny pipes, spun like a thread, and woven into stockings or cloth.

May

Flowers are blooming in the parks, in the woods, on window sills, and on spring hats. Spring peepers sing from the marsh shrubs and robins warble from apple trees. Row upon row of seeds have already gone into the garden and some are sprouting. Bees are making honey in the south. Birds are feeding fledglings in the north.

MAY DAY

THE FIRST day of May is called May Day. On that day boys and girls pick tiny wildflowers, or make little paper ones, and put them in baskets. Then they hang them on doorknobs, ring the bell, and run away. They hide near by and peek out to see how surprised and happy the people are when they open the door. You can have a lot of fun making May baskets of colored paper. Who knows, someone may hang one on your doorknob, too!

Why not have a May Day party? It is the most fun if all the children are dressed like flowers. You can make a pretty flower dress out of crepe paper, cheesecloth, or even paper napkins if you are careful. But you do not need to be dressed like a flower to feel like one. You can decide what kind of a flower you would like to be, and be one. If you have a yellow dress, you can be a daffodil, or a dandelion, or a yellow violet. If your dress is pink, you might be a pink or a petunia. The boys can be tiger lilies, snap dragons, Dutchman's breeches, or English ivy. Of course there are roses and bluebells, and all kinds of other flowers to have at the party, too.

To make this May Day like a real old-fashioned one, you should have a Maypole. Choose a tree or laundry pole, decorate it with colored paper, and fasten the ends of long paper streamers high above your head. Have each person take the loose end of one streamer, until you are all standing in a circle with the Maypole in the center.

Now you are ready for your Maypole Dance. You can run and skip, and sing and dance around the pole just as people have as long as anyone can remember.

When the streamers are wound tightly around the pole from dancing in one direction, just turn around and go the other way and they will unwind again.

MOTHER'S DAY

MOTHER'S DAY is in May also, the second Sunday in May. That is a special day when children and grownups do all kinds of nice things to show their mothers how much they love them. Sometimes they tiptoe around the house early in the morning so Mother can sleep late. They may even help Father get the breakfast and surprise Mother when she gets up. Very often even the smallest children get washed and dressed all by themselves as a surprise for Mother on this day. Sometimes they pick wildflowers and hang them in a basket on Mother's door. Sometimes they draw or paint a pretty picture for her to hang on the wall, or make little kittens or turtles or rabbits out of clay.

Best of all, they try to remember all day long that this is the day to do what Mother would like to do—to listen when she asks a question, to step quickly when she makes a suggestion. Every other day of the year Mother does things all day long for everyone else in the family. This is a very special day when everyone tries to do everything that he can for her. Of course this shouldn't be the only day to do things for Mother. Every day should be like that. But this is a good day to start thinking of Mother first.

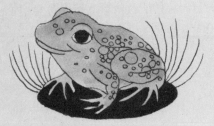

Spring Peepers

OUT IN the parks and the woods everything is green and full of life. The woodpeckers play a merry tattoo on the trees and the spring peepers sing gaily night and day. At first they sound like birds, but if you listen very carefully and then follow the song you will find a tiny little frog with very big feet and a big balloon on his throat. For when the peeper peeps, his throat swells like a balloon.

No one would ever guess to look at that little frog with his bright eyes and his lovely voice that a year ago he looked just like a piece of tapioca. In fact, if you had seen him then, you would not have known he was a frog at all. He was just a little black dot in a little round egg rolled up with a hundred others in a mass of jelly in the pond.

As the days passed things began to happen. Soon he was a tiny round ball no longer, but a long black wiggler that looked a little like a worm rolled up. Then he wiggled out from the jelly and swam away—a polliwog. He had a head, two eyes, a mouth and a tail. He looked a little like a fish without any fins.

For several days the polliwog swam around; then more changes began to take place. He felt some bumps, two up near his head and two back near his tail. Soon those bumps became little legs, and his tail began to disappear. Next thing that polliwog knew, he wasn't a polliwog any longer —he was an honest-to-goodness frog!

He had no tail at all. His tail had gradually shrunk and shrunk until there just wasn't any left.

A frog can hop out of the water onto the land. That was one of the first things he did. Since this particular little frog was a spring peeper, he could even climb bushes and trees. On each toe of each big foot, he has a little cup that helps him to stick to whatever he stands on. So up in the tree he sits. During his second spring he learns to sing, and he sings night and day, almost like a bird.

Garden Time

WHILE THE spring peepers are singing and the wildflowers are blooming, that is the time to start your garden. In a window box you can have pansies and petunias, or nasturtiums, or even candytuft. The candytuft doesn't grow candy, but it looks almost good enough to eat.

If you have a little piece of ground you can have a real garden. In it you could have marigolds and daisies, or ice plants and snow on the mountain.

Perhaps you'd like to plant something you can eat. How about parsley and mint, and beans and beets, and carrots and radishes?

First you will want to mark off the spot that is to be your garden. Put a stick in each corner. Then pull out all the grass and weeds. You will need a shovel and a rake to mix up the soil and get it nice and smooth and fine.

Now put up a stick or two sticks with a string between to mark each row. When you have the rows marked, you are ready to put in the seeds.

Be sure to have some one help you read the directions on the package. They may say to make a little trench or ditch for the seeds, or maybe you are supposed to stick your finger into the ground and then drop the seed down to the bottom of that little hole. Over some seeds you put the soil down gently, and over others you press it down very firmly with a board. You will want to be sure to do it right, because that will help the seeds to grow.

Once the seeds are planted, you will just have to wait for them to sprout. It will seem like a long wait, but it may be just a few days. Down under the dirt something is happening, even though you cannot see it.

First the moisture in the ground softly seeps into the skin of the seed to make it soft. Then the skin or jacket quietly begins to split. It has to do this to let the little plant out.

Slowly a tiny finger-like end begins to push out, then a second. The root end goes down and the plant end goes up. The root goes down into the earth to get water and minerals and good

things to feed the plant. The plant goes up toward the air and the sunlight, for the plant needs them to help it grow, too.

The first thing you see is the little plant cracking open the dirt and pushing its head out into the sunlight. Two little green leaves usually unfold out of a tight little sack, almost as though they were wrapped in cellophane. Then two more appear.

The leaves grow larger and the stem grows taller. Pretty soon you can tell what the plant is going to look like. The carrots have fuzzy, lacy tops, and the beets have very red veins in dark green leaves. The first leaves of the parsley look just like grass, but the next leaves are ragged and fringed like those we are used to eating.

Ducks' Ditty

All along the backwater,
Through the rushes tall,
Ducks are a-dabbling,
Up tails all!

Ducks' tails, drakes' tails,
Yellow feet a-quiver,
Yellow bills all out of sight
Busy in the river!

Slushy green undergrowth
Where the roaches swim—
Here we keep our larder,
Cold and cool and dim.

Every one for what he likes!
We like to be
Heads down, tails up,
Dabbling free!

High in the blue above
Swifts whirl and call—
We are down, a-dabbling
Up tails all!

KENNETH GRAHAME

May Flowers

OUT IN the meadows and the fields and the woods, when May comes, the blue, yellow, and white violets are in bloom. Many of their blossoms hide under the heart-shaped leaves, but some have longer stems and the flowers are up above the leaves. Jack-in-the-pulpits stand solemnly about the woods these days too. They have handsome green and brown striped awnings over their heads. These keep Jack dry when it rains. Jack may have one or more leaves growing on either side of him like three-part umbrellas. Near by Jack may be other three-lobed leaves that look very much like him at first. But as you look closely you will see a white or a red flower at the center of these leaves. They are the trilliums or Wake-robins and they often grow right beside the Jack-in-the-pulpits.

There may be anemones and hepaticas and May apples and bloodroot and partridgeberry and wild ginger in the woods, too.

At this time of year in the eastern United States the forsythia bushes look like great splashes of sunshine, the dogwood's white flowers hang like a mist in the woods, and the pinkster and azaleas fill parks and lawns with cascades of beautiful pinks and dazzling reds. The florists' windows are full of pretty daffodils and iris.

Baby Birds

IN MAY, too, many birds are watching over eggs in their nests. The mother bird sits on the eggs to keep them warm. Sometimes she is hungry and wants to go out and get a worm or a fly or a seed (depending on what she likes to eat). Then the father bird may keep the eggs warm for her.

One day the baby bird cracks open the shell with his special shell-cracking tooth. He is very funny-looking. His head is big and his bill is enormous. He has almost no feathers and his little legs are so weak he cannot even stand on them.

He is glad to stay quiet and warm under his mother's warm soft feathers, but he does get hungry. Then he wiggles around and opens his enormous bill until some one feeds him.

It keeps father and mother bird busy feeding him and his brothers and sisters. All day long they cheep-cheep. All day long the father and mother bird fly about getting food.

The mother and father feed the babies so well that they grow very fast. Pretty soon the nest is too small for them. One day, usually some weeks after he came out of the shell, one of the little birds hops out onto a branch and tries to fly away. He may be able to fly the very first time he tries, or he may have to exercise his wings and fly and hop a little at a time.

The rest of the nestlings soon follow him. In fact, sometimes the mother bird pushes them out of the nest when she thinks it is time for them to fly.

As soon as they are off the nest the young birds do many things. They seem to know how to get their food, how to get a drink from the little pools of rain water, how to go to sleep sitting on a bough of a tree, and how to sing as their fathers before them have sung and their father's father and their great grandfathers since time began.

June

June is a magic month. Baby rabbits hop about and fuzzy ducklings take their first swims on the pond. Little calves and long-legged colts follow their mothers wherever they go. Tiny spotted fawns lie hidden in the ferns while the mother deer nibbles young buds and tender twigs. Roses and strawberries grow wild.

FLAG DAY

THERE IS a day in June when you will see many American flags, blowing from flagpoles, hanging from people's windows, and tacked on front doors. For June 14 is Flag Day, the day we celebrate our "Stars and Stripes." It was on a day in June 'way back in 1777 that the government (it was called the Continental Congress, then) said, "The flag of the United States shall be of thirteen stripes of alternate red and white with a union of thirteen stars of white in a blue field." The thirteen stars and the thirteen stripes were for the thirteen colonies.

As the years went by people moved west over the mountains and across the plains. Gradually new states were made out of the new territory. Today all the land in the United States is divided into forty-eight states. So there are forty-eight stars on the flag—one for each state. There are still just thirteen stripes to remind us of the brave little colonies who started the Union so long ago.

Strawberries

IN JUNE the wild strawberries are beginning to ripen and the garden strawberries are at their best. Wild strawberries grow on a low plant with three small leaves on a stem. There will be some tightly closed little green buds and some wide-open flowers with five white petals and a yellow center. Then there will be some luscious, ripe, red, long strawberries. For the wild strawberries are longer than the garden strawberries in relation to their width. They are often shaped like the last joint of your little finger.

Where there are lots of strawberries there are usually strawberry festivals. You can have your own strawberry festival if you have a box of strawberries or even a jar of strawberry jam. Ask some of your playmates over for a little party. Put the jam on crackers for tarts. Fresh strawberries are good with sugar and cream or on ice cream! But they are best of all just eaten by themselves, nibbled off their stems.

The Big Dipper

WHEN the sun goes down on nights in June, the sky is full of bright stars. Some of them make pictures that are very easy to see. Probably the most famous and the most important is the Big Dipper or the Big Bear. It is a very large star picture, made of very bright stars. It is always over in the north, and it can be seen at almost any hour of the night, any night of the year, all over the United States.

Four stars make the cup of the dipper and three make the handle. On June nights the Dipper is almost exactly overhead in the top of the sky. When you have found the Dipper, you may be able to see the Bear. You need more stars to make a picture of the Bear—but if you look hard, you will see it.

The Indians used the Dipper to tell both time and direction. Sailors and woodsmen use it that way today. So the Dipper is often called the sky clock and the sky compass.

A Compass

You know a compass tells the directions—north, south, east, and west. The Dipper always tells where the north is. To find the north with the Dipper, *pretend* to draw an *imaginary* line from the end of the handle around through the bowl. Now run that imaginary line from the bottom of the bowl (on the side away from the handle) to the top of the bowl and run the line out five times that distance. There is a bright star. You can see this on the star map if you can't stay up late enough to see it in the sky. This bright star is the north star. Some people call it the pole star or north-pole star. That is because it hangs just over the north pole of the earth.

When you face toward the north, your back is toward the south. Then your right side is toward the east and your left side toward the west. The Dipper is a compass because it shows where north is, and from that you can find south, east, and west.

A Clock

The Dipper is a clock because it tells the hours of the night. Of course you won't be able to stay up all night to watch it, but astronomers have, so we know what it does. You remember that the earth spins like a top, all day and all night, never stopping. As the earth spins, it makes the sky seem to spin over our heads. So up in the north of the sky the Dipper seems to whirl around the pole star every night just as the rim seems to go around the hub of a wheel. Of course the sun is so bright in the daytime that we cannot see the stars. But at night when it is dark we can watch the Dipper. As the hours go by it measures them off.

On June evenings the Dipper hangs almost overhead in the sky. But as the hours pass it seems to be dropping down. By midnight it has dropped halfway toward the rooftops and the hills on the eastern horizon. (The horizon is where the ground seems to meet the sky as far as the eye can see.) Just before the sun comes up it has dropped 'way down to where it is resting on the horizon as though someone had set it on a table.

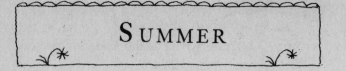

SUMMER

SUMMER begins in June. The days are long and warm. The sun rises 'way to the north of east and has a long trip across the sky. It is very high at noon. In fact, on June twenty-first it reaches as high in the sky as it ever climbs in the northern half of the world. The sun's warmest rays on that day shine on the Tropic of Cancer. That is an imaginary belt around the earth that is north of the equator.

You remember that the equator divides the earth into two equal halves, the northern hemisphere and the southern. And on this day in June the sun's straight warm rays shine right down on the tropic of Cancer in the northern hemisphere. That line goes through Havana in Cuba, Calcutta in India, Hong Kong in China, and through Mexico, too. The people who live in these places see the sun exactly overhead in the top of the sky on that day. But it is only part way up our sky because we live farther to the north over the curved surface of our big earth.

TROPIC OF CANCER

While the sun is shining warmest and longest for people in the northern half of the world, it is just the opposite in the southern hemisphere. Down in Australia and Chile and South Africa it is winter. The days are short and the sun is low in the sky.

As the world rolls on around the sun and its warm rays shift over the earth's surface this will change. The long days and the warm sun will gradually roll south again and in December when people in the north have winter, it will be summer in Australia and Chile and South Africa. So everything is pretty evenly divided.

Twenty Froggies

Twenty froggies went to school
Down beside a rushy pool.
Twenty little coats of green,
Twenty vests all white and clean.

"We must be in time," said they,
"First we study then we play;
That is how we keep the rule
When we froggies go to school."

Master Bull-frog, brave and stern,
Called his classes in their turn,
Taught them how to nobly strive,
Also how to leap and dive;

Taught them how to dodge a blow,
From the sticks that bad boys throw.
Twenty froggies grew up fast,
Bull-frogs they became at last;

Polished in a high degree,
As each froggie ought to be,
Now they sit on other logs,
Teaching other little frogs.

GEORGE COOPER

Games to Play

Of course you always play games at a party before you have the refreshments. What games would you like to play?

One good game to play is Bottle Drop. For this you need a heavy straight chair, a milk bottle, and five clothespins. You put the bottle back of the chair. Then you get up in the chair, either on your knees or standing in it if the chair is a heavy, strong one. The idea is to hold the clothespins just under your chin, then drop them one by one into the bottle. It is quite a trick.

Count the number of pins each child gets in and have him remember. This number is his score. Take two or three turns around. Then see who has the highest score. That person is the winner of the game.

A good sitting-down game is I Went On a Trip. All the players sit in a circle and the first one says, "I went on a trip and I took _____," and names one object. The second says, "I went on a trip and I took _____ and _____," naming the first player's object and adding another. Each player in turn goes through the whole list and adds one. If you skip an item or mix up the order, you are out of the game.

June is a fine time to go for a visit to the zoo, or to a farm, or to some friend's home in the country. You can go exploring and discover all kinds of fascinating things.

A trip to a museum is fun, too. There will be so many things to see that you will not be able to see them all, or remember them. You might decide to look for just special things—for little children in the pictures, or flowers, or animals. You may see a painting of a boy holding a rabbit with a little pink nose. Or you may find a statue of a little girl with a kitten. There may be a painted turtle trying to turn over that looks so real you may want to go and help him.

Hail

Some day when you are out of doors you may be surprised to have it suddenly rain iceballs. It does that sometimes, in hot weather. If you are outside you will want to run and get under something because sometimes the hailstones are as big as golf balls. Usually they are smaller than marbles, but even those sting when they hit you.

These were once raindrops that started to fall down like any raindrops. Suddenly along came a big gust of wind that whirled them high up into the colder air. As they went up they gathered more moisture and that moisture froze in the cold air up high.

Then the frozen drops started down again and along came another gust of wind that tossed them high into the colder air once more. On the way up they picked up more little particles of moisture that froze on the outside once again. Then down they started to fall.

Perhaps this time they really got way down to the ground and hit your house on the roof, or your dog on the tail, or some little boy on the head, or some little girl on the foot. As the hailstones fall they bounce off the grass, crack in pieces on the sidewalk, rattle like bullets on a tin roof, and sometimes even dent the tops of automobiles.

CUMULUS

Clouds

THERE are cloudy days in June too. It is fun to watch the clouds. They make all kinds of pictures. Sometimes down by the rooftops or off on the hilltops you will see clouds that look like great white powder puffs. These are the cumulus clouds. Then higher in the sky the wind blows clouds into trailing scarves. These are the cirrus clouds. And sometimes the sky is covered with layer upon layer of stratus clouds that look like a giant birthday cake.

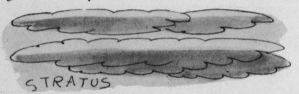

STRATUS

At other times the sky seems covered with pillows laid row on row almost like candy in the candy shop or bread on the bakery shelves. Sometimes it is overlaid with tiny clouds one over the other like the scales of a fish.

CIRRUS

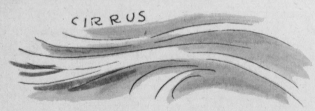

As the winds blow through the upper air they break up these cloud pictures and make new ones all the time. You can see sheep and elephants, castles and bridges on some days. At other times you can imagine a herd of horses rushing across the sky, or pick out changing faces in the slower-moving clouds.

Clouds are made of tiny particles of moisture, the same moisture that gathers together to make raindrops. Clouds are the storehouses for the rain.

The First Butterflies

THE GREAT SPIRIT thought, "By and by I will make men, but first I will make a home for them. There shall be mountains and prairies and forests, and about it shall be the blue waters of the sea."

As the Great Spirit had thought, so he did. He gave the earth a soft coat of green. He made the prairies beautiful with flowers. The forests were bright with birds of many colors, and the sea was the home of wonderful sea creatures. "My children will love the prairies, the forests, and the seas," he thought, "but the mountains look dark and cold. They are very dear to me, but how shall I make my children go to them and so learn to love them?"

Long the Great Spirit thought about the mountains. At last, he made many little shining stones. Some were red, some blue, some green, some yellow, and some were shining with all the lovely colors of the beautiful rainbow. "All my children will love what is beautiful," he thought, "and if I hide the bright stones in the seams of the rocks of the mountains, men will come to find them, and they will learn to love my mountains."

When the stones were made and the Great Spirit looked upon their beauty, he said, "I will not hide you all away in the seams of the rocks. Some of you shall be out in the sunshine so that little children who cannot go to the mountains shall see your colors." Then the south wind came by, and as he went, he sang softly of the forests flecked with light and shadow, of birds and their nests in the leafy trees.

"Dear south wind," said the Great Spirit, "here are some beautiful things for you to bear away with you to your summer home. You will love them, and all the little children will love them." At these words of the Great Spirit, all the stones before him stirred with life and lifted themselves on many-colored wings. They fluttered away in the sunshine, and the south wind sang to them.

So it was that the first butterflies came from a beautiful thought of the Great Spirit, and in their wings were all the colors of the shining stones he did not wish to hide away.

from *Book of Nature Myths* by Holbrook

The Enchanted Garden

AROUND THE garden was a low wall. The garden was divided into two parts by a path. To the right of the path was the vegetable patch and to the left were the bushes and the fruit trees. At the entrance, on either side of the iron gate, stood two old chestnut trees.

This garden, like all the gardens in the world, was enchanted. Many seeds were buried in the ground, and at the end of several weeks, the seeds changed into carrots, cabbages, salads, parsley. Under Nature's magic wand everything changed. Almost every minute there was something new. Five little spotted eggs were magically transformed into five little birds. An ugly grub turned into a beetle glistening with gold; a hairy crawling caterpillar changed into a beautiful butterfly.

And every morning, while the children of the night slept and while the birds were bursting their tiny throats with singing, the gardener pushed back the squeaky iron gate.

His two little boys came with him. One pushed the wheelbarrow and one carried the big rakes. They laughed under their big straw hats as they helped their father at his work.

But all the work of these brave little gardeners would be useless if it were not for the Good People of the garden. Every day and all day, all over the world, gardeners may dig and spade, turn over the earth and water it; they may sow the seeds, plant the cabbages, and prune the trees as much as they like—nothing would happen without the help of the Good People.

Without them, all the roots, the buds, the flowers, the fruits, the leaves and branches would be eaten up by the caterpillars, worms, grubs, and all the insects which crawled or flew everywhere.

It is the Good People who keep constant watch, day and night, over all the things that grow.

In this garden the mole was one of these. He hunted in his underground passageways, tracking down the two most terrible bandits of the garden: the mole-cricket and the white-worm, the root-cutter.

All day the swallow caught moths, flies, and midges on the wing. And in the evening the bat came to relieve him.

In the daytime, the titmouse, the nightingale, the warbler, the redbreast and their cousins protected the trees and flowers and made war on caterpillars, worms and the green fly.

The gray lizard always guarded the wall and the trellis.

When the night came, the shrew-mouse went over her rounds, while the toad stood sentinel by the old well, and the hedgehogs, a whole family of Good People, hunted the insects and ate them.

from *Spiky the Hedgehog*, by Lida

The Star-Spangled Banner

FRANCIS SCOTT KEY   18 Century English

Oh— say, can you see by the dawn's ear-ly
On the shore dim-ly seen thro' the mists of the

light, What so proud-ly we hail'd at the twi-light's last
deep, Where the foe's haugh-ty host in dread si-lence re-

gleam-ing; Whose broad stripes and bright stars, thro' the
pos - es, What is that which the breeze, o'er the

per-il-ous fight, O'er the ram-parts we watch'd, were so
tow-er-ing steep, As it fit-ful-ly blows, half con-

gal - lant-ly stream-ing? And the rock-ets' red
ceals, half dis-clos-es? Now it catch-es the

glare, the bombs burst-ing in air, Gave—
gleam of the morn-ing's first beam, In full

proof thro' the night that our flag was still there.
glo - ry re-flect-ed now— shines on the stream.

REFRAIN

Oh— say, does that star-span-gled
'Tis the star-span-gled ban-ner, oh,

ban-ner yet wave, O'er the land— of the
long may it wave, O'er the land— of the

free, And the home of the brave?
free, And the home of the brave.

[50]

July

Everyone thinks of the Fourth of July when the month of July begins. It is a holiday that everyone celebrates—the mailman, the meat man, the baker, and the grocer. Flags fly and bands play. There are parades and picnics, hay-rides and watermelon parties. Fireworks explode noisily, and at night sparklers and skyrockets shine and burst and soar.

FOURTH OF JULY

ALL THE excitement is because our country really started on the fourth of July in 1776, when the Declaration of Independence was signed. Many important projects have been started on July 4 since then. The Erie Canal was started on July 4 in 1817. And the Baltimore and Ohio Railroad was started on July 4 in 1828. Many important things have happened in July.

The Atlantic cable was successfully laid in July in 1866. It is a big rope-like bundle of wire that goes under the ocean all the way from the United States to England and makes it possible for us to telegraph and telephone across the ocean.

VACATIONS

IN JULY many people go off on their vacations, to the country, to the woods, to the lakes, to the mountains, to the seashore. Some people stay at home and do some of the things they haven't had time to do when they were busy working.

Everyone enjoys his vacation in his own way.

At the SEASHORE

IF YOU go to the seashore you will want to sit in the sand and make castles and walls and towers and dikes. You will walk along the shore to pick up sea shells. There will be red ones and yellow, white ones and blue—and all the colors of the rainbow. There will be flat and round, long and short, single and double shells. Each shell was once the home of a soft little animal, perhaps a scallop, or a conch, or a clam, or a periwinkle.

Crabs

YOU MAY see crabs scuttling across the beach, or digging in or out of their holes in the sand. If you are very quiet, the crab may go right on working while you watch him. He will disappear down his hole. Then a few seconds later you may see him just peeking over the edge. If he thinks everything is safe up there, he may back out of his hole lifting a tiny round ball of sand, then another, and another. Before long there will be a regular mound of sandballs at the entrance to his sand hole. But if you move quickly he will disappear down in the hole. He may not look out again until you are tired of waiting and have gone away.

Look carefully if you see a shell walking. It may be a hermit crab in his borrowed house. The hermit crab has no shell of his own but he is very soft all over and really needs one for protection. So he shops around until he finds an empty shell that fits him, and then wears it just as proudly as you please.

Bed in Summer

In winter I get up at night
And dress by yellow candle-light.
In summer, quite the other way,
I have to go to bed by day.

I have to go to bed and see
The birds still hopping on the tree,
Or hear the grown-up people's feet
Still going past me on the street.

And does it not seem hard to you,
When all the sky is clear and blue,
And I should like so much to play,
To have to go to bed by day?

ROBERT LOUIS STEVENSON

Learning to SWIM

AT THE shore or a lake you can learn to swim. It is really very easy to learn, and everyone wants to be able to swim. Of course you must have someone with you, always, when you are near the water. And always be very careful to do just as they say.

There are several things that you can learn about swimming right on dry land. The first is how to breathe. Most people think that the best way to breathe when you are swimming is *in* through your *mouth* and *out* through your *nose*. You can sit right in the house in a chair and begin to swim! Just breathe in through your mouth and then out through your nose.

The next thing is to learn to kick. You can kick either like a frog, bringing both legs out at the sides, and then down straight together, or like a dog, with legs straight out, kicking one at a time, fast. You can practice this lying on the bed or across a footstool.

When you get to the water, wade out (remember always to have someone with you) to knee-deep water. Turn and face the shore. Now kneel down on your knees and put your hands on the bottom. Stretch your legs out behind and begin to kick. You will discover that it is hard to stay in the same place. Your kicking makes you move through the water. Try kicking and putting one hand before the other on the bottom. This is rather as though you were walking on your hands with a motor pushing you from behind, and is one step toward learning to swim.

Of course there are many ways to swim and many, many things to learn about having fun in the water. The most important thing is not to mind when you get your face wet. Then you can have fun whatever you do. And always remember that some older person must be with you when you are in the water.

In the WOODS

IF YOU go to the woods for vacation, you will want to learn to know the flowers and the trees, the birds and the bees and the butterflies. You will discover that there are dozens, yes, even hundreds, of little animals and insects in even a small patch of the woods.

Little ants and beetles go quietly along the ground. Other bugs and insects go up and down the tree trunks. Caterpillars and worms make their way under the leaves. Birds fly in and out and up and down all around you. A bee whizzes by bound for his hive after getting the honey from the flowers. A butterfly dips softly down to light upon a leaf or blossom.

If you sit still in the woods you may see a field mouse, or a rabbit, or a squirrel. A spotted salamander or a red eft may blink his bright eyes at you from behind a rock. A land turtle may go by with his shell like a house over his back. A toad may sit and stare at you and then go hop, hop, hop out of sight.

A quick striped chipmunk may jump off a fallen log and flick his pretty tail at you. You may see him put a nut or seed into his cheek and go on to pack another into his other cheek. He may even come over to see if you have anything for him. He's a very pretty fellow and willing to make friends, if you are careful not to frighten him.

Snakes are Friends

SLIDING along silently through the grass or over the leaves may come a striped garter snake paying you a call. He has no legs, you know, and moves by wiggling from his head to his tail. He moves so smoothly all the way from head to tail that he just seems to flow along the ground. Usually you will see him with his dark eyes shining and his little forked tongue darting in and out. He uses his tongue as a tester to tell him what is going on around him.

Snakes are pretty creatures and do much good for us. They destroy insects and eat rats and mice.

Most snakes are good friends to man, but there are a few that are harmful. The best way with snakes, as with any kind of wild creature, is to stand still; they will go on and leave you alone.

A Flower Collection

HOW ABOUT making a collection of flowers? When you pick a blossom for your collection be sure to have a long stem and some of the leaves as well as the blossom itself.

Put the flowers in between sheets of newspaper to dry. Put a book or a board on top of the paper to help the flowers dry flat. It will take a day or two for them to be really dry, and you must be very careful if you touch them while they are drying.

Mount each flower on a sheet of fresh paper, and have some older person write the names beneath the flowers for you. You might put the place where you found them, and perhaps the date. Then as you collect more wildflowers you will be able to remember and to tell people what they are and where they came from.

If you go to the seashore, you can collect shells. You can carry them home in a box. Perhaps later at home you can get some cardboard and tie them into place. Then have someone write the name of each shell beneath it.

The Brook

I come from haunts of coot and hern,
    I make a sudden sally,
And sparkle out among the fern,
    To bicker down a valley,

By thirty hills I hurry down,
    Or slip between the ridges,
By twenty thorps, a little town,
    And half a hundred bridges.

I chatter over stony ways
    In little sharps and trebles,
I bubble into eddying bays,
    I babble on the pebbles.

With many a curve my banks I fret
    By many a field and fallow,
And many a fairy foreland set
    With willow-reed and mallow.

I chatter, chatter, as I flow
    To join the brimming river,
For men may come and men may go
    But I go on forever.

I wind about and in and out,
    With here a blossom sailing,

And here and there a lusty trout,
    And here and there a grayling.

And here and there a foamy flake
    Upon me as I travel
With many a silver waterbreak
    Above the golden gravel.

I steal by lawns and grassy plots,
    I slide by hazel covers;
I move the sweet forget-me-nots
    That grow for happy lovers.

I slip, I slide, I gloom, I glance
    Among my skimming swallows;
I make the netted sunbeam dance
    Against my sandy shallows.

I murmur under moon and stars
    In brambly wildernesses;
I linger by my shingly bars;
    I loiter round my cresses,

And out again I curve and flow
    To join the brimming river,
For men may come and men may go,
    But I go on forever.

ALFRED, LORD TENNYSON

THE CAT

HAVE YOU got a cat? asked the little girl on skates of the man who was leveling off fresh cement in the sidewalk.

I got a great big cat, said the man, and it says Miouooo.

The little girl looked down at the man who was on his hands and knees, working swiftly with the trowel, smoothing off the surface of the soft cement. She thought it was wonderful about the big cat, and the way the man mioued was really excellent. He might be the big cat himself, on his hands and knees.

Miouoo, he said, miouooo, and he lifted his head like a cat letting out a mournful cry.

He wasn't joking either. That was the best part of it. She liked the cat very much.

Is it a good cat? asked the little girl.

It is good sometimes, he said, and sometimes it is very bad.

When is your cat a good cat? asked the little girl.

When it catches a mouse, said the man.

When is it a bad cat? asked the little girl.

When it doesn't, said the man, smelling the sea and feeling youthful and happy.

The little girl thought about this a long time for her, ten seconds or eleven, while the man, waiting for another question, said:

Miouooo, miouooo.

How does the cat catch the mouse? asked the little girl.

Well, said the man, first the cat hides. Then the mouse comes out. Then the cat grabs the mouse and then it's goodbye mouse.

Goodbye? said the little girl.

Goodbye, said the man.

Goodbye! said the little girl.

Sure, said the man. The cat eats the mouse.

Does it hurt? asked the little girl.

I guess it hurts the mouse all right, said the man. It doesn't hurt the cat, though, he said. The cat likes it. Miouoo, he said.

A little boy arrived on skates and stopped beside the little girl.

What are you making? he asked the man.

I'm repairing the sidewalk, said the man.

He's got a big cat, said the little girl to the little boy, and it catches mice.

What's its name? asked the little boy.

Tiger, said the man.

Miouoo, said the little girl.

That's right, said the man. Miouooo, miouooo.

Miouoo, said the little boy.

Without a word the little boy and the little girl skated away together, saying miouoo.

The job was just about finished. He smoothed off a small area of fresh cement and stood up, staring toward the sea, enjoying the clean smell. He put his implements into a canvas sack and walked up a block to get the N car and return to the city. When the little boy and the little girl returned he was gone. They stood together looking down on the nice work he had done. The sidewalk was nice and clean with no broken places.

He did that, said the little girl. The man with the cat.

from *The Little Children* by William Saroyan

August

The summer days are at their hottest when August rolls around. The sun shines on the white puffs of cotton in the south and the hot air browns the leaves of the tobacco drying in the sheds. The corn is tasseled out on the plains and the grapes are coloring in the north. Gardens are heavy with tomatoes and squash, and orchards with ripening fruit.

The Corn Dance

August the Indians called the "green corn moon" because most of the corn ears were well formed by then and some were ready to eat. Corn is very important to many of the Indians—especially to the Pueblo Indians of the Southwest. These are the Indians who live in big adobe or mud apartment houses in New Mexico and Arizona. Their pueblos are hundreds of years old.

Every year, to help make sure that they will have a good crop they have a ceremonial Corn Dance. They do this because they feel that the music and singing, the costumes and the other preparations for the ceremony will please the powers that make the plants grow—the rain and the sun and the soil. The Indians believe this so seriously that the Corn Dance is like a service in church.

Early in the morning the dance begins. First several of the head dancers go through the streets of the pueblo singing. Then people come from the church carrying some of the sacred furniture into a shelter at the end of a big open street, the plaza, where the dance will be held. Then from down at the other end of the plaza the drums begin. *BOOM BOOM* boom boom. *BOOM BOOM* boom boom. Then the singers appear and start to sing. Finally the dancers come out of their sacred round rooms called the kivas.

They are dressed in beautiful costumes. The men have feathers in their long hair, and evergreen branches in their arm- and leg-bands. They wear hand-woven kilts and handsome belts, coyote skins and turtle shells.

Their bare chests and backs, arms and legs glisten in the sun and their long black hair rises and falls as they move to the steps of the dance.

The women dancers have high headdresses like rainbows and clouds. On their dark costumes quarters and nickels sparkle in the sun. Their tall white moccasins flash against the sand of the plaza and their waving evergreen plumes keep time to the endless beating of the drums.

Two by two these handsome dancers come down the center of the plaza to the beat of the drums. *BOOM* boom boom boom. *BOOM* boom boom boom. They weave and turn, circle and cross. The singers sing and sing without stopping for a minute. The drums boom continuously and never pause.

The dancers go on hour after hour. The hot sun beats on their heads and on the sand at their feet. The drum beats on the air until the boom seems to be part of every breath you take. Noon comes and goes—one o'clock, two o'clock, three o'clock. *BOOM* boom boom boom. Weave and turn, circle and cross. *BOOM* boom boom boom.

Finally at sundown the dancers file away. The singers stop. The drums cease. But in the air for hours the beat of the drum seems to linger.

The Corn Dance is a prayer, a prayer set to music, a prayer danced to song. It is a prayer for rain and sun to make the corn grow, a prayer for corn to feed the children and all the people of the pueblo.

Very often it does rain at sundown when the dance is ended, or in the morning when the music has died away. It is very easy to believe that the singing and the drumming and the dancing have helped to bring the rain.

Night

The sun descending in the west,
The evening star does shine;
The birds are silent in their nest,
And I must seek for mine.

WILLIAM BLAKE

HARVEST TIME

AUGUST is a very busy month in the country. All kinds of crops are getting ripe—beans and tomatoes, peppers, plums, and peaches. It takes thousands of people to pick all the vegetables and fruits as they ripen in the farms and orchards of the country. Many of them go to market. Others go into the cellars and storehouses of the farms. Some go to the canneries. Some are frozen. Some are dried. For there are millions of people in cities who need fruit and vegetables all through the year.

The farmers on the great plains of the Middle and Far West must harvest their wheat and barley and oats and rye. Tons and tons of the ripe grain seeds will go to the mills to be ground into flour to make bread and cakes. The flour is shipped to the stores, and the stores sell it to housewives and bakers.

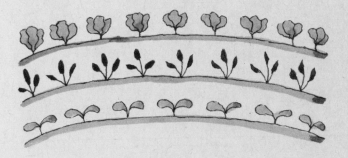

All over the country people with small gardens of their own are picking their good things to eat. When there are extra beans and tomatoes and carrots and corn, they can them at home. They may hang onions up to dry, and press apples into cider and grapes into grape juice. Perhaps they will salt down cabbage into sauerkraut.

Today we can buy fresh fruits and vegetables all year round. When our grandmothers were young things were different. Everyone had to prepare carefully for the winter, for there weren't many stores and they didn't have very many things to sell. Today fruits and vegetables can be had all year, shipped from California and Florida, from Texas and from Mexico. Refrigerator cars carry them safely long distances, and some fancy foods even come by plane.

Spiky and the Gypsies

THE WOODS were calm and safe, but there were so many new things to see and smell and hear and eat that Spiky the hedgehog wasn't a bit sleepy, although it was noon.

At the edge of the woods he met something new. A red and blue wagon with dirty curtains had stopped on the side of the road. Gypsies sat around in a circle right in the middle of the road, while a thin old horse grazed in a ditch nearby. The gypsies travelled everywhere in the wagon.

Spiky was so surprised he didn't know whether to go forward or backward. Before he could decide, a loud voice called from the caravan, "Romo! Get the wood!"

Spiky was frightened. He rolled himself into a ball.

A young boy got up slowly, walking as though he were half asleep or too lazy to move.

"Oh! Oh! Look!" he shouted all of a sudden.

His bare foot came down on Spiky's sharp-pointed back, but he was so excited he forgot the hurt and yelled at the top of his lungs, "A hedgehog! A big one! Come quick!"

"Bravo, Romo! Bravo!" called the gypsies and they all jumped up.

An old woman rushed out of the house-wagon as though her friends would eat this hedgehog raw, needles and all, before she could get there.

"Good! Good!" she cried. "Tara, run get some clay."

"Roast him on the spit!" cried one of the men. "It's quicker!"

"No! No!" screamed the old woman. "Baked in clay—tastes better. Go along, Romo, get the wood!"

Spiky didn't understand what they were saying, but he knew he was in danger.

"I'll stay rolled up, I'll stay in a ball, in a ball, in a ball," he whispered over and over again.

The old woman pushed through the cheering, laughing crowd with a pitcher of water. She poured the water over Spiky. Swish! That was the end of everything—he straightened out, as all hedgehogs are bound to do if anyone pours water on them.

A big brown hand picked him up, now that he couldn't defend himself, and a voice cried just above his head, "He is young and nice and fat!"

Just then, Spiky tried with all his might and rolled himself back into a ball! With a cry the old woman threw him into the wagon and went off giggling.

The men were making a fire. She came up to them to light her pipe.

Spiky knew that now he was alone. Very cautiously he unrolled himself. Through the door he could see the shining green grass! What luck! He crept softly to the sill and peered over. It was high off the ground! There were steps to go down but what good are they to a hedgehog? Spiky took the most direct way. Rolling himself into a ball he rolled right off the top step onto the grass below, and once he hit the ground he ran away from there as fast as his little legs could carry him. When Tara came back with the clay, Spiky was already hiding in the woods under a pile of leaves.

The gypsies were very angry and screeched at the top of their lungs when they found he had escaped.

When it was quite dark, Spiky returned safely to the garden and heaved a great sigh of relief.

from *Spiky, the Hedgehog*, by Lida

SHOOTING STARS

SOME DAY in August you may suddenly see a bright flash in the sky. The streak of light might last long enough for you to say "Mickey Mouse" and "Donald Duck" together. In August the earth runs into some sky fireworks. All through the year there are occasional shooting stars. But around the tenth and eleventh of August especially, many meteors or "shooting stars" are visible, sometimes right in the daytime, and often at night.

At this time the earth moves through a mass of hard, dark particles that get hot, shine brightly, and burn up as they go through the earth's air. The earth runs into some of these every hour of the day and night all through the year. But there are always more of them along in August.

Once there was a big comet. A comet's head is a hard, dark mass that shines when it comes near the sun. When we see comets from the earth they often look like huge stars with long shining tails out behind them. Once in a while a comet breaks to pieces, and that is what happened to this one.

All the little pieces still move through space in a big band. Once each year the earth goes right through that place in space, and we bump into the pieces of the old comet.

The pieces come into the air high above the clouds, high above the mountains, high above the highest that an airplane has ever flown. They rush through the air and go so fast that they get hot and burn up. Most of them burn up before we see them. Some get far enough down through the air so we can see them from the earth. Then we say, "Oh! A shooting star!" Or "Oh! A meteor."

Some of them do occasionally fall to earth, though no one has ever been hit by one. They

look like dark pieces of iron or stone. It seems hard to imagine that they were once beautiful, flashing, shining lights above our heads. Many of those that have fallen have been put in museums. So some day you may be able to see one.

The War Dance of the Mice: an Indian Story

ONCE upon a time there was a war between the people of Isleta and the Mice. There was a great battle, in which the Tée-wahn killed many Mice and took their scalps. Then the Tée-wahn returned to their village, and the warriors went into the *estufa* (sacred-council chamber) to prepare themselves by fasting for the great scalp-dance in twelve days. While the warriors were sitting inside, the Mice came secretly by night to attack the town, and their spies crept up to the *estufa*. When all the Tée-wahn warriors had fallen asleep, the Mice came stealing down the big ladder into the room, and creeping from sleeper to sleeper, they gnawed every bowstring and cut the feathers from the arrows and the strap of every sling. When this was done, the Mice raised a terrible war-whoop and rushed upon the warriors, brandishing their spears. The Tée-wahn woke and caught up their bows and arrows, but only to find them useless. So the warriors could do nothing but run from their tiny foes, and up the ladder to the roof they rushed pell-mell and thence fled to their homes leaving the Mice victorious.

The rest of the town made such fun of the warriors that they refused to return to the fight,

and the elated Mice held a public dance in front of the *estufa*. A brave sight it was, the army of these little people, singing and dancing and waving their spears. They were dressed in red blankets, with leather leggings glistening with silver buttons from top to bottom, and gay moccasins. Each had two eagle feathers tied to the top of his spear—the token of victory. And as they danced and marched and countermarched, they sang exultingly:

"Shée-oh-pah ch'-ot-un!
Nah-mah - hlee - oh ch'-ót-im!
Hlo'-tu feé-ny p'-óh-teh!"

over and over again—which means

Quick we cut the bowstring!
Quick we cut the sling strap!
We shaved the arrow-feathers off!

For four days they danced and sang, and on the night of the fourth day danced all night around a big bonfire. The next morning they marched away. That was the time when the Mice conquered men; and that is the reason why we have never been able to drive the Mice out of our homes to this day.

from *Pueblo Indian Folk Stories* by Charles F. Lummis

September

September days are sunny and brisk. There is the last of summer in the air and the first of fall. The long days of June and July have been gradually shortening. The short nights of July and August have been lengthening. As the days and nights grow more nearly the same length, we can be sure that fall is at hand.

THE FALL EQUINOX

EVERY DAY the sun is highest in the sky at noon.

The summer sun is very high at noon.

The winter sun is very low, even at noon.

The noonday sun in spring and fall is midway up our sky.

On September 23 there are twelve hours of night and twelve hours of day. They are equal once again. September 23 is the day of the fall equinox. Remember? Equinox means equal night and day. Once again the sun rises exactly east and sets exactly west, and down at the earth's equator the sun is overhead at noon.

From now on the earth will move on around the sun and the warm straight rays of the sun will be shining down below the equator onto the southern half of the world. Up north the sun's rays will be so slanting and have so far to go through the earth's thick blanket of air that the earth will grow colder day by day.

Down in the southern hemisphere the days will grow longer and warmer. People in Australia will be having spring and getting ready for summer while people in England and the United States are having fall and getting ready for winter.

The people who live near the equator are warm all the year round because the warmest, straightest rays shine on that part of the earth all the time.

The sun is not the only thing which affects our climates. Warm and cold ocean currents are important, too. Some places in the United States, like Florida, never get very cold because they are quite far south and near warm water. California is also warm in winter because it is near a warm ocean current. But Maine and Massachusetts are cold in winter because the ocean they are near has cold currents instead of warm.

Labor Day

THERE IS a holiday in September to celebrate the importance of work. It is called Labor Day, and it is a holiday all over the country. Most people have to do some kind of work. Some people are farmers and raise wheat or corn or cows or pigs, or cotton or sugar or vegetables or fruits. Some people are miners and dig coal and copper and iron and tin and gold and lead out of the earth. Some people are factory workers and make cars and trains and boats and airplanes. Some are merchants and sell clothes and food and furniture and tools. Some are architects and carpenters, and bricklayers and plumbers. Some are truck-drivers and train men, sailors, and aviators. Some work in banks and some sell insurance. There are doctors and lawyers, dentists and nurses. There are so many interesting things to do that every boy and girl will be able to work at something he likes when he grows up.

Years ago, families grew their own food, built their own houses, made their own shoes and clothes, and did everything for themselves. Some people still do that today. But most people learn how to do one thing well and they are paid for that. With the money they earn they pay for the things they need—a place to live, food to eat, clothes to wear, and books to read.

La Fayette

HOW WOULD YOU like to have a name like this—Marie Joseph Paul Yves Roch Gilbert du Motier, Marquis de La Fayette? That is the name of a famous September-born Frenchman who was a very good friend to America.

When La Fayette was nineteen years old he heard that the thirteen colonies in America were fighting for their independence from England. La Fayette was so interested in this struggle that he had a ship built and sailed across the ocean with some friends to offer their help to General Washington.

They did help the Americans, and later La Fayette returned to France and persuaded the king to send twelve hundred soldiers, who were a great help in winning the war.

La Fayette has been a hero to Americans ever since.

September

*Apples heavy and red
Bend the branches down,
Grapes are purple
And nuts are brown,
The apples smell sharp and sweet on the ground
Where the yellow bees go buzzing around.
And way up high
The birds fly southward
Down the sky.*

MARGARET WISE BROWN

The Sandman

The rosy clouds float overhead,
  The sun's going down;
And now the sandman's gentle tread
  Comes stealing through the town.
"White sand, white sand," he softly cries,
  And so he shakes his hand,
Straightway there lies on babies' eyes
  His gift of shining sand.
Blue eyes, gray eyes, black eyes, brown,
  As shuts the rose, they softly close,
When he goes through the town.

From sunny beaches far away—
  Yes, in another land—
He gathers up at break of day
  His stores of shining sand.
No tempests beat that shore remote,
  No ships may sail that way;
His little boat alone may float
  Within that lovely bay.
Blue eyes, gray eyes, black eyes, and brown,
  As shuts the rose, they softly close,
When he goes through the town.

He smiles to see the eyelids close
  Above the happy eyes;
And every child right well he knows—
  Oh, he is very wise!
But if, as he goes through the land,
  A naughty baby cries,
His other hand takes dull gray sand
  To close the wakeful eyes.
Blue eyes, gray eyes, black eyes, and brown,
  As shuts the rose, they softly close,
When he goes through the town.

So when you hear the sandman's song
  Sound through the twilight sweet,
Be sure you do not keep him long
  A-waiting in the street.
Lie softly down, dear little head,
  Rest quiet, busy hands,
Till, by your bed, his good-night said,
  He strews the shining sands.
Blue eyes, gray eyes, black eyes, and brown,
  As shuts the rose, they softly close,
When the sandman goes through the town.

MARGARET THOMSON JANVIER

[66]

Use Your Eyes

Do you know anyone who cannot see? Have you often wondered how they could tell who you were and what was happening around them? If you are blindfolded you will discover that you can *almost* see with your ears and with your hands and with your mind.

Some people who cannot see make beautiful rugs, write books, make cakes, and do all kinds of things. They have learned to use their ears and their hands and their minds instead of their eyes. Sometimes they notice more of what is going on around them than people do who can see with their eyes but do not use them well.

The Mole

There is a little animal that cannot see, but lives a very busy and useful life. He is the mole. He has a long, strong nose, big, sturdy front feet, silky gray fur, and a naked little pink tail.

He burrows under the lawn and the garden eating worms and grubs and beetles. Very seldom does he come out on top of the ground, but sometimes you can see the top of his tunnels pushing up little ridges in the grass.

When he does come out he goes back in very quickly. He puts down his nose, pushes his big front claws up beside it, and bores in. Then he uses his front claws to pass back the dirt to his hind feet. It doesn't take him more than a flash to disappear right out from under your very nose.

Do you think that you could dig a trench deep enough to lie in and twice as long as you are tall in an hour, even if you had a shovel and a hoe? The mole has only his claws for tools, yet he can dig six times his own length in an hour. He can go 100 feet in a day. He is a very hard worker, and most of the time he is busy getting rid of troublesome worms and insects, which makes him a help to us in garden and field.

Come, Little Leaves

"Come, little leaves," said the wind one day.
"Come over the meadows with me and play;
Put on your dresses of red and gold
For summer is gone and the days grow cold."

Soon as the leaves heard the wind's loud call,
Down they came fluttering, one and all;
Over the brown fields they danced and flew,
Singing the sweet little song they knew.

"Cricket, good-by, we've been friends so long,
Little brook, sing us your farewell song;
Say you are sorry to see us go;
Ah, you will miss us, right well we know.

"Dear little lambs in your fleecy fold,
Mother will keep you from harm and cold;
Fondly we watched you in vale and glade,
Say, will you dream of our loving shade?"

Dancing and whirling, the little leaves went,
Winter had called them, and they were content;
Soon, fast asleep in their earthy beds,
The snow laid a coverlet over their heads.

GEORGE COOPER

The Wraggle Taggle Gypsies, O!

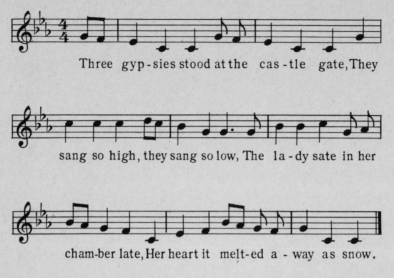

Three gyp-sies stood at the cas-tle gate, They sang so high, they sang so low, The la-dy sate in her cham-ber late, Her heart it melt-ed a-way as snow.

They sang so sweet, they sang so shrill,
   That fast her tears began to flow.
And she laid down her silken gown,
   Her golden shoes and all her show.

She plucked off her high-heeled shoes,
   A-made of Spanish leather, O.
She would in the street, with her bare, bare feet;
   All out in the wind and weather, O.

O saddle to me my milk-white steed,
   And go and fetch me my pony, O!
That I may ride and seek my bride,
   Who is gone with the wraggle taggle
     gypsies, O!

O he rode high, and he rode low,
   He rode through wood and copses too,
Until he came to an open field,
   And there he espied his a-lady, O!

What makes you leave your house and land?
   Your golden treasures for to go?
What makes you leave your new-wedded lord,
   To follow the wraggle taggle gypsies, O?

What care I for my house and my land?
   What care I for my treasure, O?
What care I for my new-wedded lord?
   I'm off with the wraggle taggle gypsies, O!

Last night you slept on a goose-feather bed,
   With the sheet turned down so bravely, O!
And tonight you'll sleep in cold open field,
   Along with the wraggle taggle gypsies, O!

What care I for a goose-feather bed,
   With the sheet turned down so bravely, O?
For tonight I shall sleep in a cold open field,
   Along with the wraggle taggle gypsies, O!

October

When October comes the days are shorter and cooler. The grasses in the north are turning brown and many of the flowers are gone. The seeds of plants sail about on the breeze like tiny silken parachutes. Corn shocks stand around like Indian tepees with yellow pumpkins ripening for Halloween. The air is full of the smoke of autumn fires and smell of burning leaves. It's time to gather nuts in the south.

HALLOWEEN

Halloween comes on October 31. It is the day for jack-o'-lanterns and witches on broomsticks and ghosts in sheets and all kinds of strange doings. This holiday comes at a time of year when people all through history have been accustomed to celebrating. The American Indians used to have special dances then, the Romans honored their goddess of the harvest, Pomona, and the Druids in ancient England held special rites. Our Halloween today is a mixture of all these old celebrations.

Jack-o'-Lanterns

Having a jack-o'-lantern is the most fun of all on Halloween, and the very best ones are those you help make yourselves, from round orange pumpkins. First cut a circle out of the top, so you can lift off the cover by the stem. Then hollow out the inside. Now you are ready to cut the face—eyes, nose, and funny mouth for candlelight to shine through. Last of all a grownup will help you drop wax in the bottom of the jack-o'-lantern and set a stubby candle firmly in the wax to burn brightly after dark.

Masks

Dressing up in funny masks and costumes is great fun, too. You can make your masks of paper. Draw a funny face about the size of your own, and color it with crayons to look like a witch or goblin or any funny character. Run a long string through a little hole on each side of the mask and leave the ends long enough so you can tie it in back. Cut holes for your eyes and nose and mouth, and slip the mask into place. Now look at yourself in the mirror!

Costumes

You can be a fine GHOST if Mother will lend you an old sheet for the evening and help you wrap it around you, over your head and draped around your arms, too, so that you will be completely covered—with just your white mask showing. Be careful not to trip over your robes, though!

To be a WITCH you will need a broomstick to ride, a mask to cover your face, shawl over your shoulders, and a pointed black hat. You can make the witch's hat by sewing together with big stitches two sheets of heavy black construction paper, twisting them into a cone, stitching or pinning them into shape, and cutting the bottom smooth.

A GYPSY costume is good for Halloween too. Borrow bright scarves to wear around your waist and shoulders, and around your head for a turban. Borrow lots of old beads from your mother or big sisters and wear lots of bright jewelry.

A Halloween Party

MAYBE you can get permission to have an evening party for Halloween. Have the guests come into a dark room and let them follow a string draped from doorknobs and chairs to lead them to the room where you will play games.

BOB FOR APPLES afloat in a big tub of water. Players are not allowed to use their hands, but must bite the apple to get hold of it. Apples can be hung from strings, too, and players can stretch to reach the apple and bite it. Any player who gets hold of an apple gets it to eat.

BLINDFOLD DETECTIVE is a good game, too. One player is blindfolded and has to tell who each of the others is just by hearing their voices. Or you can play it keeping quiet, with the detective feeling gently of faces, hair, and clothing for "clues."

FORTUNE-TELLING. Have a grown-up help you write "fortunes" enough for all your guests on small pieces of paper. Put all these into a big kettle, perhaps over an imitation fire of sticks and red crepe paper. Have a "witch" preside over the kettle, and have all the guests march by, each taking a folded fortune from the kettle. Then have them all sit in a circle and read the fortunes aloud.

At Night

After we're tucked in bed at night,
    As usual, much too soon,
Mother pulls the curtains back
    So we can see the moon.

The moon is glad to shine for us.
    But if she's still in bed
Or much too young to come herself,
    She sends a star instead.

MARCHETTE GAYLORD CHUTE

Preparing for the Winter

NOT FAR FROM the oak tree Quick the Squirrel stopped.

He started to scratch the earth under a bush. When he had made a little hole, he put a nut in, and covered it with earth and pine needles.

The squirrel children, thinking it was a game, hid their nuts also in the ground.

But it wasn't a game.

Father Quick was a wise squirrel. He knew that when the hazel nuts were gone it would grow colder and colder. The sun would come up late and set early. The wind would blow through the forest, and one day the snow would start to fall from the sky.

The snow is white and soft, but very cold. It covers all the earth.

Quick had already seen all that and he knew that then there would be no more foods for the squirrels. So, like all far-seeing squirrels, the Quicks started to store away provisions.

They hid pine cones, beechnuts, hazelnuts, and mushrooms in old nests and in the hollows of trees, to keep them dry and good. They buried them under bushes and under stones.

As soon as their meal was finished, they went to work filling little larders all over the forest.

The wind had already begun to blow, and the water in the stream was as cold as ice.

The leaves of the hazelnut tree turned yellow and fell to the ground, and the Quick children were as big as their father and mother.

And then one day the snow started to fall.

Slowly, slowly, the little white stars came from the sky, and the young squirrels watched with wonder. It was their first snow. It fell faster and faster, and soon all the countryside was white.

And the squirrel children thought sadly of the warm sunshine, the green grass, and the flowers.

No one told them, but they knew in their little squirrel hearts that the world would not always be so white and cold. They knew that the trees would turn green and that the sun would shine brightly again.

They were cold, so they nestled close to one another and went peacefully to sleep.

from *Pompom, the Little Red Squirrel* by Lida

The Wind

I saw you toss the kites on high
And blow the birds about the sky;
And all around I heard you pass,
Like ladies' skirts across the grass—
  O wind, a-blowing all day long,
  O wind, that sings so loud a song!

I saw the different things you did,
But always you yourself you hid.
I felt you push, I heard you call,
I could not see yourself at all—
  O wind, a-blowing all day long,
  O wind, that sings so loud a song!

O you that are so strong and cold,
O blower, are you young or old?
Are you a beast of field and tree,
Or just a stronger child than me?
  O wind, a-blowing all day long,
  O wind, that sings so loud a song!

ROBERT LOUIS STEVENSON

Fog

The fog comes
On little cat feet.

It sits looking
Over the harbor and city
On silent haunches
And then moves on.

CARL SANDBURG

Autumn Fires

In the other gardens
And all up the vale,
From the autumn bonfires
See the smoke trail!

Pleasant summer over
And all the summer flowers,
The red fire blazes,
The gray smoke towers.

Sing a song of seasons!
Something bright in all!
Flowers in the summer,
Fires in the fall!

ROBERT LOUIS STEVENSON

OVER THE PARKS and fields in October it is sometimes very foggy, just as though a cloud were on the ground instead of high over our heads in the sky. That is really what fog is—a cloud on the ground. It is made of tiny particles of moisture hanging in the air.

Sometimes the fog hangs down between the buildings in the city and all around the trees all day, especially near the ocean or near a river or a lake. It may drift up in the noonday sun, or it may just gradually disappear in the late afternoon. There may be the smell of smoke in the air. For in late October when the leaves are falling from the trees in the north there are many bonfires, and the fog keeps the smoke from climbing up into the air.

Long ago there were huge bonfires out on the plains. Their smoke could be seen and smelled for hundreds of miles. That was when there were herds of buffalo, and the Indians sometimes lighted the prairie grass to help drive the buffalo where they could kill them.

Nowadays there are very few buffalo left and very few Indians on the plains. But there are still prairie fires, and the clouds of smoke fill the whole sky and make the sun look like a huge red ball of fire. And we still call those days in October when it is warm and the sun hangs like a red ball in the October haze "Indian summer."

The Pasture

I'm going out to clean the pasture spring;
I'll only stop to rake the leaves away
(And wait to watch the water clear, I may):
I shan't be gone long.—You come too.

I'm going out to fetch the little calf
That's standing by the mother. It's so young,
It totters when she licks it with her tongue.
I shan't be gone long.—
  You come too.

ROBERT FROST

Indian Summer

The Indians come in the autumn.
Their war paint is in the trees;
The haze is the smoke of their peace pipes
As they settle and take their ease.
The shocks of corn are their tepees;
And the feathers that fall from their hair
Drift like leaves into bunches
And lie to be scuffled there.

MARCHETTE GAYLORD CHUTE

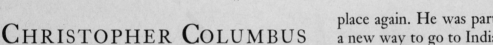

CHRISTOPHER COLUMBUS

SOME FOUR HUNDRED and fifty years ago, in 1492, Christopher Columbus set out to sail around a world he knew was round. There were many people in his day who thought he could not do it. They thought the world was flat and if he went very far on the ocean he would fall off the edge of the world.

Of course the world does *look* flat. That is because people are so small and the world is so big. It seems to stretch out like a table in all directions as far as the eye can see. But if you go to the ocean you can watch a ship come up over the curve of the earth's round surface. First the mast or smoke-stack appears, later the lower part of the ship can be seen. When a ship sails away it seems to roll over the curved edge of the earth, too.

Columbus had been to sea, and had noticed this. He had listened to the astronomers, too, who were sure that the earth was round. They had seen its shadow on the moon. They had even measured its size. Still many people found it hard to believe that the earth was a round ball some 8,000 miles through and about 25,000 miles around.

Columbus believed that he could start out, keep sailing in the same direction, and finally go 'way around the earth and come back to the same place again. He was particularly anxious to find a new way to go to India, where there were valuable spices and silks.

Finally he got three ships and men to sail them. He sailed and sailed and sailed and sailed. His men began to worry. They thought they should sight land. They thought that Columbus did not know what he was doing. They wanted to go back home.

Finally they did sight land. It was an entirely new part of the world, that no one had ever heard of. Columbus had discovered the new land which we now call America. Columbus never did sail all the way around the world, because America got in his way. But because he did sail across the ocean and discover a new continent that no one in Europe knew was there, we celebrate Columbus Day on October 12, the day of his first landing in America.

There were people and plants and animals in the new world unlike any in the old world. Columbus took back some of the people, whom he called "Indians." You see he still thought that he must have reached some part of the India he had set out for. He took back corn; no one in Europe had ever seen that. He took tobacco; that was new to them too. And he took pumpkins and a variety of other plants and strange things from this strange new world.

WINTER IN THE WOODS

(Mole, lost in the wintry Wild Wood, is now at Mr. Badger's home. His friend Water Rat has found him there.)

THE FRONT-DOOR bell clanged loudly, and the Rat, who was very greasy with buttered toast, sent Billy, the smaller hedgehog, to see who it might be. There was a sound of much stamping in the hall, and presently Billy returned in front of the Otter, who threw himself on the Rat, with an embrace and a shout of affectionate greeting.

"Get off!" spluttered the Rat, with his mouth full.

"Thought I should find you here all right," said the Otter cheerfully. "They were all in a great state of alarm along River Bank when I arrived this morning. Rat never been home all night—nor Mole either—something dreadful must have happened, they said; and the snow had covered up all your tracks, of course. But I knew that when people were in any fix they mostly went to Badger, or else Badger got to know of it somehow, so I came straight off here, through the Wild Wood and the snow! My! it was fine, coming through the snow as the red sun was rising and showing against the black tree trunks! As you went along in the stillness, every now and then masses of snow slid off the branches suddenly with a flop! making you jump and run for cover. Snowcastles and snow-caverns had sprung up out of nowhere in the night—and snow bridges, terraces, ramparts—I could have stayed and played with them for hours. Here and there great branches had been torn away by the sheer weight of the snow, and robins perched and hopped on them in their perky conceited way, just as if they had done it themselves. A ragged string of wild geese passed overhead, high on the grey sky, and a few rooks whirled over the trees, inspected, and flapped off homewards with a disgusted expression; but I met no sensible being to ask the news of. About half-way across I came on a rabbit sitting on a stump, cleaning his silly face with his paws. He was a pretty scared animal when I crept up behind him and placed a heavy forepaw on his shoulder. I had to cuff his head once or twice to get any sense out of it at all. At last I managed to extract from him that Mole had been seen in the Wild Wood last night by one of them. It was the talk of the burrows, he said, how Mole, Mr. Rat's particular friend, was in a bad fix; how he had lost his way, and 'They' were up and out hunting, and were chivvying him round and round. 'Then why didn't any of you *do* something?' I asked. 'You mayn't be blest with brains, but there are hundreds and hundreds of you, big, stout fellows, as fat as butter, and your burrows running in all directions, and you could have taken him in and made him safe and comfortable, or tried to, at all events.'

" 'What, *us?*' he merely said; '*do* something? us rabbits?' So I cuffed him again and left him. There was nothing else to be done. At any rate, I had learnt something; and if I had had the luck to meet any of 'Them' I'd have learnt something more—or *they* would."

"Weren't you at all—er—nervous?" asked the Mole, some of yesterday's terror coming back to him at the mention of the Wild Wood.

"Nervous?" The Otter showed a gleaming set of strong white teeth as he laughed. "I'd give 'em nerves if any of them tried anything on with me. Here, Mole, fry me some slices of ham, like the good little chap you are. I'm frightfully hungry, and I've got any amount to say to Ratty here. Haven't seen him for an age."

So the good-natured Mole, having cut some slices of ham, set the hedgehogs to fry it, and returned to his own breakfast, while the Otter and the Rat, their heads together, eagerly talked river-shop, which is long shop and talk that is endless, running on like the babbling river itself.

from *The Wind in the Willows* by Kenneth Grahame

November

November days are frosty and November nights are long. The orchards are bare and the gardens are spaded up for next year. Winter wheat is in the ground and the birds have started south. Lofts and root cellars bulge with winter stores. The squirrels and mice have laid in their winter supply of nuts and seeds. The turkeys are fattening for Thanksgiving.

The north wind doth blow,
And we shall have snow,
And what will poor robin do then, poor thing?
He'll sit in the barn
And keep himself warm,
And hide his head under his wing, poor thing.

The north wind doth blow
Bleak in the morning early;
All the hills are covered with snow,
Cold winter's come now fairly.

A Great Inventor

THOMAS EDISON loved his work so much that he didn't even want to stop to sleep or eat. He did many wonderful things. Some of the things he did have made a great difference in the life of every boy and girl and every grown-up. For Thomas Edison developed the incandescent electric light, the motion picture, the phonograph, and many other things we use every day.

It was on a day in November in 1877 that Edison was able to record a person's voice on a tin-foil disc and then play it back through the horn of his phonograph. As the voice went down through the horn, its sound was scratched into the turning tin-foil disc by a needle.

What Thomas Edison said into the horn was, "Mary had a little lamb." Then he lifted the needle out to the starting edge and turned the disc round once again.

This time the voice came back through the horn. Out came the words, "Mary had a little lamb." After that it was possible to have voices, pianos, and whole orchestras recorded.

Edison was an inventor. He worked in a laboratory and workshop. But most of all he worked in his mind. He looked about him and he thought about what he saw.

When he had an idea he examined it from every side. He didn't say, "Oh, that could never be done." He worked at it. And dozens and dozens of times he found out that it could be done. The result was that he was able to invent all kinds of useful machines and devices that we use every day.

THANKSGIVING

WHEN NOVEMBER comes the harvest is in. The farmer is thankful for his good crops. Down in the root cellar are carrots and cabbage and turnips and squash. Out in the barn the hayloft is overflowing with sweet-smelling grasses and clover. Silos are full of the juicy winter food for the cattle. Bins are full of golden oats for the horse. Corn cribs are bulging with drying ears for the pigs.

Up in the attic braids of onions hang from the rafters, and baskets of apples are lined up on the floor. High in the cold peak of the roof hang ducks and pheasants with their feathers still on—just the way the hunters brought them in. Near by may be a saddle of venison and some bacon still fragrant from the smoke-house.

The cellar and the attic, the cupboard and the pantry bulge with stores of food. It is no wonder that Thanksgiving is celebrated in November. We give thanks that there is food to eat, thanks that there are relatives and friends to share it with us, thanks that we are well and happy.

The Pilgrims first celebrated Thanksgiving. They had wild turkey, and goose, mince pie, nuts, and all kinds of good things. Today we still have turkey and goose and mince pie and nuts and all kinds of good things to eat.

Of course it is a good idea to be thankful on other days besides Thanksgiving. Some people give thanks before every meal. Many people say a prayer every night before going to bed, for there are many things to be thankful for every day. We should be thankful that we can see and hear, that we can speak and walk and run, thankful to have families and friends, we should be thankful to be able to play games and to go to school some day, to have toys and books, to have warm homes and clothes. There are many, many things that we are thankful for when we stop to think about it.

When you stop to think how lucky you are, perhaps you will think of some children who are less fortunate than you are. Some are cold and hungry. Some are sick and lonely. Some do not have enough clothes. Some have no toys and no books.

Do you suppose that there are any toys that you could spare to send to them? Have you a book that you do not look at often any more? Do you have a pair of shoes that you do not need any longer or a coat that is too small for you? Think about it and ask your family if they would help you pick out something to send to the children at the settlement house or at the hospital.

It is fun to share your things, to make other people happy. Then you will be living by the Golden Rule: "Do unto others as you would have them do unto you." This means that you should think how you would like to have people treat you, and then treat them in the same way.

You will find that if you remember to say "Thank you" and "You are welcome," people will be more polite to you. If you listen when people speak to you, they will be more likely to listen when you talk to them. Remember to walk quietly when others are asleep and you will discover that they will tiptoe silently about when you are resting. You can make a game of being polite. Being polite and thoughtful is fun for everyone, young and old.

DANNY MEADOW MOUSE *Plays Hide and Seek*

LIFE IS always a game of hide and seek to Danny Meadow Mouse. You see, he is such a fat little fellow that there are a great many other fur-coated people, and almost as many who wear feathers, who would gobble Danny up for breakfast or dinner if they could. Some of them pretend to be his friends, but Danny always keeps his eyes open when they are around and always begins to play hide and seek. Peter Rabbit and Jimmy Skunk and Striped Chipmunk and Happy Jack Squirrel are all friends whom he can trust, but he always has a bright twinkling eye open for Reddy Fox and Billy Mink and Shadow the Weasel and old Whitetail the Marsh Hawk, and several more, especially Hooty the Owl at night.

Now Danny Meadow Mouse is a stout-hearted little fellow, and when rough Brother North Wind came shouting across the Green Meadow, tearing to pieces snow clouds and shaking the snowflakes until they covered the Green Meadow deep, deep, deep, Danny just snuggled down in his warm coat in his snug little house of grass and waited. Danny liked snow. Yes, sir, Danny Meadow Mouse liked the snow. He just loved to dig in it and make tunnels. Through those tunnels in every direction he could go where he pleased without being seen by anybody. It was great fun.

Every little way he made a round doorway up beside a stiff stalk of grass. Out of this he could peep at the white world and he could get the fresh air. Sometimes when he was quite sure that no one was around, he would scamper across on top of the snow from one doorway to another, and when he did this he made the prettiest little footprints.

Now Reddy Fox knew all about those doorways and who made them. Reddy was having hard work to get enough to eat this cold winter. One morning as he came tip-toeing softly over the meadow, what should he see ahead of him but the head of Danny Meadow Mouse pop out of one of those little doorways. Reddy's mouth watered, and he slid forward more softly than ever. When he got within jumping distance, he drew his stout hind legs under him and made ready to spring. Presto! Danny Meadow Mouse had disappeared. Reddy Fox jumped just the same and began to dig as fast as he could make his paws go. He could smell Danny Meadow Mouse and that made him almost frantic. All the time Danny Meadow Mouse was scurrying along in one of his little tunnels, and when finally Reddy Fox stopped digging because he was quite out of breath, Danny popped his head out of another little doorway and laughed at Reddy. Of course Reddy saw him, and of course Reddy tried to catch him there, and dug just as frantically as before. And of course Danny Meadow Mouse wasn't there.

After awhile Reddy Fox grew tired of this kind of game and tried another play. The next time he saw Danny Meadow Mouse stick his head out, Reddy pretended not to see him. He stretched himself out on the ground and made believe that he was very tired and sleepy. He closed his eyes. Then he opened them just the tiniest bit, so that he could see Danny Meadow Mouse and yet seem to be asleep. Danny watched him for a long time. Then he chuckled to himself and dropped out of sight.

No sooner was he gone than Reddy Fox stole over close to the little doorway and waited. "He'll surely stick his head out again to see if I'm asleep, and then I'll have him," said Reddy to himself. So he waited and waited. By and by he turned his head. There was Danny Meadow Mouse at another little doorway laughing at him.

from *The Adventures of Danny Meadow Mouse*
by Thornton Burgess

Scrapbooks

KEEPING a scrapbook is fun, and November is a good time to start one.

Get permission to collect all the older magazines in the house, and look through them for pictures you would like to keep. You may want pictures of all kinds of things, or perhaps you will be most interested in pictures of automobiles, or of airplanes, of animals or flowers or tools or machines or houses or clothes.

Whenever it is rainy or cold outside, you can have a good time finding pictures for your book.

When you cut out the pictures for your book, be sure to pick up all the scraps, and pile the magazines neatly when you are through. Then your family will be eager to help you whenever you want to work on your scrapbook.

Put down some newspapers before you paste so that you do not get the paste on anything but your pictures and your book. It is a good idea to keep a cloth handy so that you can wipe the extra paste off your hands and off the edges of the pictures.

Keeping Healthy

THE BEST time to see the doctor is when you are feeling well. Then he can look at your eyes, and into your ears, and down your throat and up your nose. He can thump your chest and count your heart beats. He can help you to keep well and healthy.

It is good to go to the dentist, too, at least twice a year. Then he will get out his little mirror and look at the back of your front teeth and the front of your back teeth, at your upper teeth and at your lower teeth. If there are any cavities, he will fill them, and if a tooth needs to come out, he will help you to pull it.

We have just one pair of eyes and ears for all our lives. We can buy new suits and dresses, new toys and machines, but there is no store where we can get new parts of the body. So it is important to take care of ourselves. The doctors and the dentists are here to help us. Of course, mostly it is up to each one of us. Plenty of sleep and fresh air, good food and good fun, games outdoors and quiet play inside, are all important.

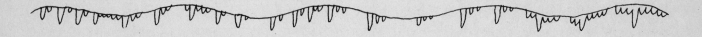

Old Sayings About the Weather

If the oak be out before the ash
The summer will be but a splash:
If the ash be out before the oak
The summer will be all a soak.

September mild, October gold,
Are followed by November cold.

Mackerel skies and mares' tails
Make great ships carry low sails.

Ice in November enough to bear a duck,
All the coming winter will be mud and muck.

An air' winter,
A sair winter.

Rain before seven,
Fine before eleven.

Between one and two
See what the day will do.

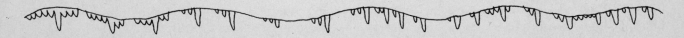

As Winter Comes

WHEN NOVEMBER draws to an end, the winter is not very far away. The animals and the birds have been well aware of this for some time. Many of the birds have already gone south. The warblers and the wrens, the grosbeaks and catbirds, the thrushes and the orioles have left the northern states and started flying south with the sun.

First a few gathered together in the park or at the edge of a wood lot. Then a few more came calling along. One by one, two by two, the number of the flock grew until there were hundreds, perhaps even thousands of the same kind of bird flying together.

Meadow larks and bobolinks, song sparrows and kinglets, they all seem to know when the days get shorter that it will be warmer if they fly to the south. So off they go, even the new little birds that hatched from the eggs just a few short months ago. They fly hundreds, sometimes thousands of miles, across lakes and rivers, even across bays and long stretches of ocean.

The geese fly in vast wedges or waveys and sometimes there are so many of them that they take hours to pass over one spot. Great numbers of ducks fly south, too, but they do not fly in such beautiful formations as the geese.

Robins and bluebirds often stay longer than some of the other birds, but some day you may hear them calling to one another, and off they will go. Pretty soon only the hardiest birds remain—the bluejays and the sparrows, the pigeons and starlings.

One of the butterflies, the Monarch, migrates to the south in winter, too. He is a large one, orange in color with black veins and edges on his wings and little white dots on the edges. When the time comes for him to fly south—some time during the autumn months, in September or early October—the butterfly flies to a bush or tree where there may be already dozens of others waiting to start south.

They wait on this bush or tree until there may be hundreds of pretty orange and black butterflies.

No one knows just how they decide when to

start or how they know where to go, but suddenly they flutter off the bush and start to fly. They move their wings slowly up and down or coast on the breeze. Then they flutter their wings again and float on the air once more. Mile after mile, over hill and dale, over river and lake they fly. Sometimes they are carried along in a high wind and sometimes they are dashed down by a heavy rain. But day after day they fly and fly southward.

In the spring they are back again. Once more we see them fluttering and floating on the air, lighting on a flower here and there.

Strange as it seems to us, the animals seem to know how to keep track of the seasons and how to know which is north and which is south. Many birds fly to the same place in the south each winter and then return to the same place in the north each summer.

Animals that have never seen a winter seem to know when winter is coming and what to do about it. Little bears born in the spring and woodchucks only a few months old seem to know just what to do. They eat very heavily all fall and store up a deep layer of fat under their skins. Then when the short, cold days of November come, they go into their burrows under the ground or into the far end of a cave, roll up, and go to sleep. They don't wake up and walk around again until the spring comes.

Now that is the way bears and woodchucks have done since time began. Their mothers and fathers, great-grandmothers and great-grandfathers did the same thing when winter came. But how the young animals know what to do, we cannot understand.

All Through the Night

Welsh Air

Sleep, my child, and peace at-tend thee, All through the night;
While the moon her watch is keep-ing, All through the night;

Guard-ian an-gels God will send thee, All through the night.
While the wear-y world is sleep-ing, All through the night.

Soft the drow-sy hours are creep-ing, Hill and vale in slum-ber steep-ing,
O'er thy spir-it gent-ly steal-ing, Vis-ions of de-light re-veal-ing,

Love a-lone his watch is keep-ing, All through the night.
Breathes a pure and ho-ly feel-ing, All through the night.

America the Beautiful

KATHARINE LEE BATES — SAMUEL A. WARD

O Beau-ti-ful for spa-cious skies, For
O Beau-ti-ful for pil-grim feet Whose

am-ber waves of grain, For pur-ple moun-tains
stern im-pass-ioned stress, A thor-ough-fare for

maj-est-ies A-bove the fruit-ed plain. A-
free-dom beat A-cross the wild-er-ness. A-

mer-i-ca! A-mer-i-ca! God
mer-i-ca! A-mer-i-ca! God

shed his grace on thee, And crown thy good with
mend thine eve-ry flaw, Con-firm thy soul in

broth-er-hood From sea to shin-ing sea!
self con-trol, Thy lib-er-ty in law!

O beautiful for heroes proved
　In liberating strife,
Who more than self their country loved,
　And mercy more than life!
America! America!
　May God thy gold refine,
Till all success be nobleness
　And every gain divine!

O beautiful for patriot dream
　That sees beyond the years
Thine alabaster cities gleam
　Undimmed by human tears!
America! America!
　God shed His grace on thee,
And crown thy good with brotherhood
　From sea to shining sea!

KATHERINE LEE BATES

WINTER

TIME PASSED, and Bambi had many adventures. Every day brought something new. Sometimes he felt quite giddy. He had so incredibly much to learn.

He could listen now, not merely hear when things happened so close that they struck the ear of their own accord. He could listen intelligently to everything that stirred, no matter how softly. He heard even the tiniest whisper that the wind brought by. For instance, he knew that a pheasant was running through the next bushes. He recognized clearly the soft tread that was always stopping. He knew by ear the sound the field mice make when they run to and fro on their little paths; and the patter of the moles when they are in good humor and chase one another around the elder bushes so that there is just the slightest rustling. He heard the shrill clear call of the falcon, and he knew from its altered, angry tones when a hawk or an eagle approached.

He knew how to snuff the air now, too. Soon he would do it as well as his mother. He could breathe in the air and at the same time analyze it with his senses. "That's clover and meadow grass," he would think when the wind blew off the fields. "And Thumper is out there, too. I can smell him plainly." From time to time, he would wake up, listen, and snuff the air to find out how things stood. Everything was as it should be. The titmice were chattering a little, the midges humming and the wood-doves cooing. Bambi would listen and then drop off to sleep again.

One morning he woke up shivering with cold. Even before he opened his eyes, his nose told him there was something new and strange in his world. And when he looked out through the thicket and saw everything covered with white, he jumped to his feet.

"It's snow, Bambi," his mother said. "Go ahead and walk out. It's all right."

Cautiously Bambi stepped on the surface of the snow and saw his feet sink down in it. He picked his feet up high as he walked, and looked around at the tracks he left in the snow.

Bambi was delighted. The air was calm and mild while the snow-stars whirled down and the world looked completely different. The sun shone on the flashing whiteness, which sparkled so brightly that it almost blinded Bambi.

Trotting slowly ahead, Bambi suddenly felt the solid earth disappear beneath his feet. He plumped into deep snow that almost covered his body. He pawed frantically until his feet touched ground and pushed him out of the snowdrift. After that, Bambi walked more carefully through the forest.

from the Walt Disney adaptation of *Bambi* by Felix Salten

November is the month in which elections are held. Election day is the first Tuesday after the first Monday in November. Then people all over the country go to the polls, as voting places are called, and cast their votes. On ballots they tell whom they want for each office.

Who Are Americans?

EVERYONE BORN in America is an American. He may have any kind of name. He may have black or yellow, white or red skin. But if he has been born under the American flag, he is an American.

And many people who were born in other countries have come to America to live. They have decided that they would like to be Americans. So they have learned to speak English, and have learned about George Washington and Abraham Lincoln and about the history of our country. Then they have asked to be made citizens of the country.

What Citizens Do

CITIZENS HELP run the country. They can vote for the mayor of their town or city. They can help to elect the governor of the State. They can vote for members of the school board, and help to decide all kinds of matters which will affect them and their children, their neighbors and their friends. They can send representatives and senators to Washington to represent them in the national government. They can vote for the president and vice-president.

From Foreign Lands

PEOPLE FROM many countries have come to live in America, and each group has brought something that has made our country a better place to live in. They have given us pictures and music, new foods and strange customs, beautiful materials and great books. These immigrants have taught us how to make and do many things.

From Greece have come expert sponge fishers, from Belgium fine lace-makers, from France famous wine-makers, from Germany master book-makers. From Italy have come wonderful singers, from China and Brazil skilled tea and coffee blenders, from Russia brilliant musicians.

Very often you can tell by a person's name where his father or grandfather used to live.

Do you know anyone who speaks French or German, Spanish or Russian, Chinese or Polish, Swedish or Portuguese? Perhaps he will tell you how to say "hello" and "good-by" in that language. Perhaps he will tell you about a foreign country in which he has lived or visited. Someday you may be able to take a trip to a foreign country. You may see strange animals and flowers, strange buildings and strange food, and hear a foreign language spoken.

OUR FRIENDS THE MICE

IN SPITE OF our cat, there were mice in our house. At night when it was very quiet and the lights were out and we were in our beds we could hear the mice coming out of their holes and running over the wood floor of our kitchen, and if we listened carefully we could hear them squeak, and it was amusing to listen to them. I thought it was very good to have these small, timid, and secretive things in our house, and I thought of them as being our mice of our house, and therefore I felt that they were a part of our life. They were thieves and they had to steal their food, but all the same they were a family, just as we were a family, and since they were living in our house with us I had affection for them.

Sometimes at night, listening to the mice, I could feel my brother Krikor listening to them with me. We slept in the same room and his bed was beside mine so that we were very close, and if I was awake in the darkness and he was awake I could feel that he was awake because it was different when he was asleep. I could feel him listening to the mice with me, and I would say, Do you hear them, Krikor? And Krikor would say, Don't talk. They will start to play now.

I had seen mouse-traps before, but I had never studied one closely, and I had certainly never thought of one in relation to *our* mice. Now we had these three mouse-traps and my sister Lucy was determined to rid our house of the mice.

Cheese was placed in the mouse-traps and they were set, and in the morning we found that two of them had caught mice but that one of them had become unset and did not have a mouse in it. The cheese was gone. My mother thought this was very strange. It must have been a very shrewd mouse, she said. I felt very happy because one of our mice had got away alive, and I had an idea this mouse returned to the other mice and said, They've got traps up there now with cheese in them. You go to get the cheese and something comes down over you and kills you. I saw it happen and it nearly happened to me, but I was too quick for it. I want you to be very careful from now on and I want you to keep your eyes open, and don't be fooled by cheese that isn't where it belongs, on a dish or on a shelf. If you see any wire on a piece of wood, stay away from it. It's a trap. It will kill you. It is better to go hungry and be alive than to get a little piece of cheese in your mouth and then be killed.

Sometime during the following night I became awake and began to listen for the mice. I listened for a little while and I heard nothing and I could feel that my brother Krikor was not awake. Then I heard a trap snap and I began to think about the mouse that was being crushed to death. In less than a minute I heard another trap snap. I wondered what had come over the mice. Why hadn't they learned to stay away from traps? Then I heard the third trap snap, and I thought, Well, at this rate, all our mice will be killed in less than a week. And I fell asleep.

Well, it was my brother Krikor. After a while he came back to our room and got in bed. I was so wide-awake by this time and I was thinking so steadily about the traps and our mice that my brother Krikor found out about my being awake. We began to whisper softly and my brother Krikor said, I went to fix the traps. We don't want to kill those mice with traps. I put the cheese on the floor for them and they will come pretty soon and eat it and go away. We will hear them when they come.

from *Inhale and Exhale* by William Saroyan

November

From the trees the leaves are flying
On the ground the leaves are dying
And this is the Fall of the year.
A cold rain comes down from a cold sky
On the last yellow chrysanthemums in the
    garden.
The rain makes the leaves all shiny
Red and yellow and purple and shiny.
The shaggy chrysanthemums in the garden
Smell their cool tiger tang smell.
Chestnuts are roasted and apples are red.
And now to give Thanksgiving
For the kindness
Of the year.

MARGARET WISE BROWN

The Fly

How large unto a tiny fly
    Must little things appear!—
A rosebud like a feather bed,
    Its prickle like a spear;

A dew-drop like a looking glass,
    A hair like golden wire,
The smallest grain of mustard-seed
    As fierce as coals of fire;

A loaf of bread, a lofty hill;
    A wasp, a cruel leopard;
And specks of salt as bright to see
    As lambkins to a shepherd.

WALTER DE LA MARE

December

December is a very special month. There are mistletoe and holly to be gathered in the south and Christmas trees to be cut in the north. The muskrats have built their winter houses and some of the animals have already started a long winter sleep. Mysterious packages are hidden in closets and dresser drawers. Christmas preparations fill the days with excitement and surprises.

December

December comes with falling snow
And a sharp cold wind begins to blow.
The white snow comes again
It falls softly in the night
White
From the dark blue sky.
It covers the earth that the spring kept green
And summer kept warm.
It covers the earth where the autumn leaves fell
Golden on the ground.
All is white
All is still
Christmas bells ring out to the cold starlit sky.
And Christmas trees shine green as emeralds
With rubies and diamonds and sapphires
The light of all the world
On Christmas night.

MARGARET WISE BROWN

The Christmas Star

LONG AGO and far away many wise men spent their lives studying the stars. One night a brilliant new star shone in the sky. Three wise men of the east saw the star and followed it to the little town of Bethlehem. There in a manger they found the baby Jesus, whose birthday we celebrate every year at Christmas.

What was that brilliant light that hung over Bethlehem so long ago? We cannot find it in the sky today. Some say it was a new star that suddenly blazed into brilliance and then died down again. Others feel that it may have been an especially bright comet, or a shooting star. It might even have been several planets, which shone close together in a great glow at the time of that first Christmas.

Many people say it was a miracle to guide the wise men to the manger in Bethlehem. Every person must choose the explanation he likes the best, for no one in the whole world knows what the Christmas star really was.

Christmas Decorations to Make

IN THE NORTHERN part of the United States and in many parts of Europe it is the custom to have a Christmas tree. Sometimes it is put on a table in the house and sometimes it is so large that it goes all the way from the floor to the ceiling. Out in the city parks they sometimes have a tree that is as tall as a house.

When you are indoors on cold, blustery days in December you can have lots of fun making decorations for your Christmas tree, or for your house if you do not have a tree.

Popcorn Trimmings

POPCORN MAKES a fine trimming for a tree. After you have popped it, thread a big darning needle with some string. Put the needle through the kernel and string the corn just like a string of beads. If you have some cranberries they make very pretty red beads in between the popcorn kernels. When these are hung on the green tree, with colored paper chains and candy canes, nothing could look prettier. Of course colored electric lights are splendid, too.

Paper Chains

ONE OF THE prettiest things to make is a chain of paper rings. All you need for this is scissors and paste and colored paper. Cut strips about half an inch wide and three or four inches long.

Put a daub of paste on one end of a ring, loop it over, and hold it tight against the other end until the paste dries and you have one nice, round ring. Now slip the next strip of paper through the first ring, loop it around, and paste it shut in the same way. Keep going, and you can make your chain as long as you like.

Let's Make Christmas Cards

EVERYONE KNOWS it is fun to receive Christmas presents. But it is even more fun to give them, especially when you have made them yourself.

A nice gift you can make for everyone you love—Mother, Dad, sisters and brothers, and favorite aunts, uncles, and friends—is a Christmas card. You can make each one different, or you can make them all alike.

Make little books of paper just as you did for valentines. Use red and green papers for your Christmas cards. Draw a snowman and a Christmas tree. Cut them out and use them for patterns.

Try pasting a white snowman on a green card, a green Christmas tree on a red card.

Inside, a grownup will help you write your name or maybe you can write it yourself.

To make special Christmas presents of your cards, you can buy tiny calendars for about a penny, and paste one neatly inside. That present will last all year! Or you can buy a sheet of blotting paper and cut a nice clean square to paste inside your card. Grownups always need blotters.

When your cards are finished, you can paste the open edges shut with a Christmas sticker and have a grownup address the back just like an envelope.

O Little Town of Bethlehem

Rev. Phillips H. Brooks

1. O lit-tle town of Beth-le-hem! How still we see thee lie.
2. O ho-ly child of Beth-le-hem! De-scend to us, we pray.

A - bove thy deep and dream-less sleep, The si - lent stars go by;
Cast out our sin and en - ter in, Be born in us to - day.

Yet in thy dark streets shin-eth The ev - er-last-ing light;
We hear the Christ-mas an-gels The great glad tid-ings tell,

The hopes and fears of all the years Are met in Thee to - night.
O come to us, a - bide with us, Our Lord Em-man-u - el!

Silent Night, Holy Night

JOSEF MOHR   FRANZ GRUBER

pp   *mf*

Si - lent night, Ho - ly night! All is calm,

all is bright, 'Round yon Vir - gin Moth-er and Child.

Ho - ly In-fant so ten-der and mild, Sleep in heav-en-ly

pp

peace,___ Sleep __ in heav - en-ly peace!___

[91]

Beethoven

ONE OF THE greatest musicians of all time was born in December. Ludwig van Beethoven made the world a more beautiful place to live in by writing music for the piano, violin, and for whole orchestras. His music is so beautiful that everyone loves it. It has been called "the language of the human heart" because everyone can enjoy it and understand it. It seems to sing of sunshine and rain, of spring days and winter nights, of boys and girls and birds and butterflies. It is fast and slow, it is light and tender, it is dark and smooth, it is wild and stormy.

Beethoven was an unhappy little boy. He was often lonely and he did not have much chance to play with children or with toys. But he did play the piano and he loved music. He practiced at the piano for hours and hours of every day for years and years. He kept on loving music more than anything else in the world.

He could sit at the piano and make the prettiest tinkling, melodious tunes. Later he wrote the music for many instruments to play together. It was great music that marched, that soared, that sang open a door into your very heart and filled it with wonder and joy.

Would you think that anyone who could not hear could write music? Yet Beethoven was deaf. When he was twenty-eight years old he began to hear a buzzing in his ears and he found that it was very hard for him to understand people or to hear soft music. By the time he was thirty-four, he resigned himself to the fact that he would never regain his hearing. But he was sure that he could still write music. He could and he did. He wrote his most wonderful symphonies after he could not hear.

When he died in 1827, people were filled with sorrow. But his music will live forever, and people everywhere will listen to it with joy.

Christmas Around the World

CHRISTMAS IS the loveliest of holidays, and it is celebrated in ever so many different ways in different parts of the world.

Christmas cribs, with figures representing the Holy Family, the wise men, and the shepherds, are set up in homes and churches, especially in southern Europe.

In old England, children dressed in costumes went out "*mumming*" at Christmas-time. They sang carols, did dances, and sometimes even gave little plays, and in return people invited them into their homes for treats.

Caroling is still popular, and groups of children go about singing Christmas songs at their friends' homes.

Christmas trees came from Germany.

Christmas sheaves are put out for the birds in Norway and Sweden.

Huge *Yule logs* are burned on Christmas Eve in France and England.

Midnight mass is an important part of the Christmas celebration in many countries.

In Holland, France, and Spain *wooden shoes* or slippers, or *Christmas stockings* are put out by children hoping for gifts.

We enjoy many of these customs of Christmas-time which have come to us from faraway countries.

The Day after Christmas

WHEN THE excitement of Christmas is over, some of your friends and playmates may come over to pay you a visit. Are there, by chance, some tiny presents under your tree for them? Can you find some candy and nuts or some oranges and apples for them to eat? Or maybe they would like one of the candy canes hanging on your tree.

And the day after Christmas *you* may decide to go off on a round of visits to your friends. You may go to see their Christmas trees and, if they are willing, to play with some of their new toys.

And the next day after Christmas, or the next day after that, when you can still remember who gave you what presents,—you will want to write some "thank you" notes. Then the people who sent you presents will know that you received them and that you appreciate their sending them to you.

The Friendly Beasts

Jesus our brother, strong and good,
Was humbly born in a stable rude,
And the friendly beasts around Him stood,
Jesus our brother, strong and good.

"I," said the donkey, shaggy and brown,
"I carried His mother up hill and down,
"I carried her safely to Bethlehem town;
"I," said the donkey, shaggy and brown.

"I," said the cow all white and red,
"I gave Him my manger for His bed,
"I gave Him my hay to pillow His head,
"I," said the cow all white and red.

"I," said the sheep with curly horn,
"I gave Him my wool for His blanket warm,
"He wore my coat on Christmas morn;
"I," said the sheep with curly horn.

"I," said the dove, from the rafters high,
"Cooed Him to sleep, my mate and I,
"We cooed Him to sleep, my mate and I;
"I," said the dove, from the rafters high.

And every beast, by some good spell,
In the stable dark was glad to tell,
Of the gift he gave Immanuel,
The gift he gave Immanuel.

TWELFTH CENTURY CAROL

The First Airplane Flight

LONG BEFORE there were ever any airplanes, men watched the birds and tried to imitate their flying, but they never could. Finally they found a way to float on the air with a big pair of wings, but they had no way of moving through the air wherever they wanted to go.

Then one December day in 1903 a wonderful thing happened. An airplane built by two brothers named Wright, driven by a chugging motor, rose up into the air and flew along for several hundred feet before it landed. The first flight lasted less than a minute, but it proved that it could be done.

That first airplane of Wilbur and Orville Wright's paved the way for the planes nowadays which fly miles above the earth and can cross the broadest seas. They can land on water or land, and people can eat or sleep or talk to people on the ground while riding in them.

A Feeding Station for Birds

WHEN YOU are planning your Christmas tree, don't forget the birds and squirrels. It is hard for them to find food in the winter, and they will be eager for crumbs and nuts and seeds.

Early in December, fix a feeding place on a window sill or in the yard. You will be surprised how soon your bird friends will discover your feeding station and come to depend on you.

They will come every day, looking for crumbs and seeds. There will be sparrows and pigeons, perhaps cedar waxwings and chickadees. There may be nuthatches and bluejays, too. Squirrels will come, too, looking for nuts.

As a special Christmas treat, get some suet for the birds. The meat man will sell you some for a few pennies. The birds like suet very much, and it is very good for them in chilly, blustery December. When you take the trimmings off your tree, give them the popcorn and cranberries to eat, too.

The Little Bird

Once I saw a little bird
  Come hop, hop, hop;
So I cried, "Little Bird,
  Will you stop, stop, stop?"
And was going to the window
  To say "How do you do?"
But he shook his little tail,
  And far away he flew.

SONGS

STORIES

POEMS

INDEX